Identity with Windows Server 2016: Microsoft 70-742 MCSA Exam Guide

Deploy, configure, and troubleshoot identity services and Group Policy in Windows Server 2016

Vladimir Stefanovic
Sasha Kranjac

BIRMINGHAM - MUMBAI

Identity with Windows Server 2016: Microsoft 70-742 MCSA Exam Guide

Copyright © 2019 Packt Publishing

Commissioning Editor: Kartikey Pandey
Acquisition Editor: Shrilekha Inani
Content Development Editor: Ronn Kurien
Technical Editor: Aditya Khadye
Copy Editor: Safis Editing
Language Support Editor: Mary McGowan
Project Coordinator: Jagdish Prabhu
Proofreader: Safis Editing
Indexer: Pratik Shirodkar
Graphics: Tom Scaria
Production Coordinator: Deepika Naik

First published: January 2019

Production reference: 1310119

Published by Packt Publishing Ltd.
Livery Place
35 Livery Street
Birmingham
B3 2PB, UK.

ISBN 978-1-83855-513-9

www.packtpub.com

`mapt.io`

Mapt is an online digital library that gives you full access to over 5,000 books and videos, as well as industry leading tools to help you plan your personal development and advance your career. For more information, please visit our website.

Why subscribe?

- Spend less time learning and more time coding with practical eBooks and videos from over 4,000 industry professionals

- Improve your learning with Skill Plans built especially for you

- Get a free eBook or video every month

- Mapt is fully searchable

- Copy and paste, print, and bookmark content

Packt.com

Did you know that Packt offers eBook versions of every book published, with PDF and ePub files available? You can upgrade to the eBook version at `www.packt.com` and as a print book customer, you are entitled to a discount on the eBook copy. Get in touch with us at `customercare@packtpub.com` for more details.

At `www.packt.com`, you can also read a collection of free technical articles, sign up for a range of free newsletters, and receive exclusive discounts and offers on Packt books and eBooks.

Contributors

About the authors

Vladimir Stefanovic is a Microsoft Certified Trainer (MCT) and system engineer with more than 10 years of experience in the IT industry. Over his IT career, Vladimir has worked in all areas of IT administration, from IT technician to his current system engineer position. As a lead system engineer at Serbian IT company SuperAdmins and lead technician trainer at Admin Training Center, he successfully delivered numerous projects and courses. He is also an active conference speaker, having spoken at a long list of conferences, such as MCT Summits (in the USA, Germany, and Greece), ATD, WinDays, KulenDayz, and Sinergija (Regional Conferences). He is the leader of a few user groups and is an active community member, with the mission to share knowledge as much as possible.

Sasha Kranjac is a security and Azure expert and instructor with more than two decades of experience in the field. He began programming in Assembler on Sir Clive Sinclair's ZX, met Windows NT 3.5, and the love has existed ever since. Sasha owns an IT training and consulting company that helps companies and individuals to embrace the cloud and be safe in cyberspace. He is a Microsoft MVP, MCT, MCT Regional Lead, Certified EC-Council Instructor (CEI), and currently holds more than 60 technical certifications. Sasha is a frequent speaker at various international conferences, and is a consultant and trainer for some of the largest Fortune 500 companies.

About the reviewer

Mustafa Toroman is a program architect and senior system engineer with Authority Partners. With years of experience of designing and monitoring infrastructure solutions, lately he focuses on designing new solutions in the cloud and migrating existing solutions to the cloud. He is very interested in DevOps processes, and he's also an Infrastructure-as-Code enthusiast. Mustafa has over 30 Microsoft certificates and has been an MCT for the last 6 years. He often speaks at international conferences about cloud technologies, and he has been awarded MVP for Microsoft Azure for the last three years in a row. Mustafa also authored *Hands-On Cloud Administration in Azure* and co-authored *Learn Node.js with Azure*, both published by Packt.

Packt is searching for authors like you

If you're interested in becoming an author for Packt, please visit `authors.packtpub.com` and apply today. We have worked with thousands of developers and tech professionals, just like you, to help them share their insight with the global tech community. You can make a general application, apply for a specific hot topic that we are recruiting an author for, or submit your own idea.

Table of Contents

Preface

Welcome to *Identity with MCSA Windows Server 2016 Certification Guide: Exam 70-742*. This book is designed to give you a deep understanding of identity solutions in Windows Server 2016 and prepare you for Exam 70-742: Identity with Windows Server 2016, which is a part of the MCSA: Windows Server 2016 Certification. The book will start with the installation and configuration of **Active Directory Domain Services (AD DS)** and then will covers implementing and managing Active Directory services in advanced scenarios. Group Policy and GPO implementation will be explained, as well as using **Active Directory Certificate Services (AD CS)** to manage certificates in a domain environment. Finally, **Active Directory Federation Services (AD FS)** as the Microsoft implementation of federated identity will be covered, as well as **Active Directory Rights Management Services (AD RMS)** as a document protection solution will be covered.

Who this book is for

This book is aimed at anyone who wants to learn about identity in Windows Server 2016 and earn some valuable Microsoft certifications. To better understand the content of this book, you should to have knowledge of Windows Server operating systems, and experience of working with them.

What this book covers

Chapter 1, *Installing and Configuring Active Directory*, will give you deep understanding of AD DS and how to install and configure AD DS in different scenarios.

Chapter 2, *Managing and Maintaining Active Directory*, covers advanced AD DS configuration and services that are tightly related to Active Directory environments, such as Active Directory Domains and Trusts and Active Directory Sites and Services.

Chapter 3, *Creating and Managing Group Policy*, will explain you what a Group Policy is, how to configure and manage Group Policy Objects (GPOs), and how to implement GPOs in different environments.

Chapter 4, *Understanding and Implementing Active Directory Certificate Services*, explains the Public Key Infrastructure (PKI) and AD CS and covers how to implement and manage AD CS in Windows Server 2016.

Chapter 5, *Understanding and Implementing Federation and Rights Management*, covers the implementation and management of Microsoft's federated identity solution, AD FS, and Rights Management solution implementation using AD RMS.

To get the most out of this book

Before you start with this book in order to prepare for Exam 70-742, you should have understanding of Active Directory environment and related services. Experience of configuring Windows Server 2012 and Windows Server 2016 is required to better understand Active Directory-related services. The following Windows Server roles and services will be used in this book:

- Active Directory Domain Services (AD DS)
- Active Directory Domains and Trusts
- Active Directory Sites and Services
- Group Policy Management
- Active Directory Federation Services (AD FS)
- Active Directory Rights Management Services (AD RMS)
- Domain Name System (DNS)

Conventions used

There are a number of text conventions used throughout this book.

CodeInText: Indicates code words in text, database table names, folder names, filenames, file extensions, pathnames, dummy URLs, user input, and Twitter handles. Here is an example: "By default, the location of the AD DS database is C:\Windows\NTDS\ntds.dit."

Any command-line input or output is written as follows:

```
Install-WindowsFeature AD-Domain-Services -IncludeAllSubFeature -
IncludeManagementTools
```

Bold: Indicates a new term, an important word, or words that you see onscreen. For example, words in menus or dialog boxes appear in the text like this. Here is an example: "Select **Operation Masters**."

Warnings or important notes appear like this.

Tips and tricks appear like this.

Get in touch

Feedback from our readers is always welcome.

General feedback: If you have questions about any aspect of this book, mention the book title in the subject of your message and email us at customercare@packtpub.com.

Errata: Although we have taken every care to ensure the accuracy of our content, mistakes do happen. If you have found a mistake in this book, we would be grateful if you would report this to us. Please visit www.packt.com/submit-errata, selecting your book, clicking on the Errata Submission Form link, and entering the details.

Piracy: If you come across any illegal copies of our works in any form on the Internet, we would be grateful if you would provide us with the location address or website name. Please contact us at copyright@packt.com with a link to the material.

If you are interested in becoming an author: If there is a topic that you have expertise in and you are interested in either writing or contributing to a book, please visit authors.packtpub.com.

Reviews

Please leave a review. Once you have read and used this book, why not leave a review on the site that you purchased it from? Potential readers can then see and use your unbiased opinion to make purchase decisions, we at Packt can understand what you think about our products, and our authors can see your feedback on their book. Thank you!

For more information about Packt, please visit `packt.com`.

1
Installing and Configuring Active Directory

From Windows Server 2000, **Active Directory Domain Services (AD DS)** has become the default identity provider for Windows operating systems. AD DS represents a central point for authentication and management of all AD DS objects, such as users, groups, and computer accounts. The AD DS database, a central store in AD DS, stores information related to users, groups, computers, services, and all other resources in the AD DS hierarchical structure, and is also known as the directory. AD DS gives us the ability to search objects through the hierarchically organized directory structure and to apply configuration and security settings to all active directory objects.

In this chapter, you will learn why we need AD DS, the components of AD DS, how AD DS is installed and configured, and how to create and manage AD DS objects.

We will learn about the following topics in this chapter:

- Introduction to Active Directory
- Installing and configuring Active Directory
- Active Directory users and computers
- Active Directory groups and organizational units

Introduction to Active Directory

Every AD DS is composed of both logical and physical components. All components work together and each component has a specific role in the proper functioning of AD DS. In this section, you'll learn what those components are and why they're important. We'll also look at which tools can be used to manage AD DS and what's new in AD DS in Windows Server 2016.

A knowledge of logical components is important for the proper implementation of appropriate AD DS design for an organization.

The following table shows the logical and physical components of AD DS:

Logical components	Physical components
• Partitions • Schema • Domains • Domain trees • Forests • Sites • Organizational units • Containers	• Domain controllers • Read-only domain controllers • Data stores • Global catalog servers

Logical components

Logical components in AD DS are structures that are used to implement AD DS design. Different designs are appropriate for different organizations, so knowledge of logical components and their purpose is very important. In the following section, we'll describe the logical components in more detail.

Partitions

A partition is a portion of the AD DS database. Although the AD DS database stores all the data in one file, `C:\Windows\NTDS\ntds.dit`, the AD DS database is composed of a few different partitions and each partition contains different data. The AD DS database is logically separated into the following directory partitions:

- **Schema partition**: There is only one schema partition per forest. The schema partition is stored on all domain controllers in the forest and contains definitions of all objects and attributes of objects.
- **Configuration partition**: The configuration partition contains information about the forest-wide AD DS structure, as well as information about the domains and sites in a forest and the domain controllers that are installed in a forest.
- **Domain partition**: Domain partitions are stored on every domain controller in a domain and contain information about users, groups, computers, and organizational units. All objects from the domain partition are stored in the global catalog.

- **Application partition**: Every application in AD DS needs to store, categorize, and use specific information. This information is stored in the Application partition that can be domain- or forest-wide, depending on the application type.

Partitions are replicated through directory replication and are stored on every domain controller in the domain and forest.

> By default, the location of the AD DS database is `C:\Windows\NTDS\ntds.dit`. While promoting the server to a domain controller, you can define another location for the AD DS database.

Schemas

A schema defines all object classes and attributes that AD DS uses to store data. Each AD DS object has a lot of attributes that need to be populated, such as the name, `sAMAccountname`, the canonical name, and the location. All of these are controlled by the schema. All domains in a single forest contain a copy of the schema that applies to the forest level. Each change in the schema is replicated from the schema master to every domain controller in the forest. The schema master is typically the first domain controller installed in a forest. An AD DS schema can be changed or modified, but only when necessary. The schema is responsible for information-storage controls, and every untested schema change can potentially affect other applications in the forest that use AD DS. Any schema changes must be performed by the Schema Admins and from the schema master.

> Schema changes are one-way. You can't delete anything from a schema, you can only extend or modify schema attributes or classes.

> In most cases, a schema needs to be updated for specific applications. For example, if you want to install Microsoft Exchange Server 2016, you must apply the Exchange Server 2016 Active Directory schema changes. This will be done during the installation of the Exchange Server and will be performed without user interaction.

Domains

The domain is a logical component that acts as a central administrative point for AD DS objects, such as users, groups, and computers. Domains use a specific portion of the AD DS database and can be connected to other domains in a parent-child structure or a tree structure. The AD DS database stores all domain objects, and each domain controller holds a copy of the AD DS database.

AD DS uses a multi-master replication model. This means that every domain controller in the domain can make a change to the objects in the domain and that change will be replicated in all other domain controllers.

The AD DS domain provides authentication and authorization for domain-joined users. Every time the domain user wants to sign in to a domain-joined computer, AD DS must authenticate the login. Windows operating systems use authorization and access-control technologies to allow authenticated users to access resources.

Every domain in a forest has some objects that are unique to that domain:

- **Domain Admins group**: By default, every domain has an administrator account and a Domain Admins group. The administrator account is a member of the Domain Admins groups, and the Domain Admins groups is, also by default, a member of the local Administrators group on each domain-joined computer.
- **RID master role**: The **Relative Identifier (RID)** master role is a domain-specific role that's responsible for assigning a unique SID to the new AD DS object. If the RID master server isn't online, you might have issues adding new objects to the domain.
- **Infrastructure master role**: This FSMO role is responsible for inter-domain object references, when objects from one domain are part of a group in another domain. If servers with this role are unavailable, domain controllers that aren't configured as a global catalog servers won't be able to authenticate users.
- **PDC emulator role**: The **Primary Domain Controller (PDC)** emulator FSMO role is responsible for time synchronization. The PDC master is the time source for a domain and all PDC masters in the forest synchronize their time with the PDC in the forest root domain. The PDC master is a domain controller that receives information if the user changes their password and replicates that information to other domain controllers. The PDC emulator also plays a big role in editing the GPO, because a PDC holds an editing copy. This prevents potential issues if multiple administrators want to edit the same GPO at the same time.

Domain controllers don't have local users and groups, so local Administrator groups don't exist on domain controllers.

Domain trees

A domain tree is a hierarchical collection of domains in the same forest that share the same root domain name. In the domain tree structure, AD DS domains are organized as parent-child domains.

Forests

A forest is a collection of one or more domain trees that share the AD DS root domain and schema. The first configured domain in the forest is called the root domain. A forest can either contain only one domain or it can be composed of hundreds of domains in different domain trees. The root forest domain contains a few objects that only exist in the forest root domain:

- **Schema master role**: This special, forest-wide FSMO role can only exist once in a forest. As mentioned earlier, a schema can only be changed from the domain controller that holds this role.

- **Domain-naming master role**: This is another special, forest-wide FSMO role that can only exist once in a forest. The domain-naming master role is responsible for adding new domains, so if the domain controller that holds this role isn't online, new domains can't be added to the forest.

- **Enterprise Admins group**: By default, the Enterprise Admins group has the Administrator account for the forest root domain as a member. The Enterprise Admins group is the most powerful group in the forest, because it's a member of the local Administrators group in every domain in the forest. Members of the Enterprise Admins group have full administrative control in every domain in the forest.

- **Schema Admins group**: By default, the Schema Admins group has no members. Only members of the Enterprise Admins group or the Domain Admins group (in the forest root domain) can add members to the Schema Admins group. Only members of the Schema Admins group can make changes to the schema.

Every forest has security and replication boundaries. Security boundaries, by default, are very strict. No one from outside the forest can access any resources inside it. If you need to provide access to one forest from another forest, you need to configure forest trust between them. Unlike the forest security boundaries, all the domains in a forest automatically trust the other domains in the forest. With this default configuration, access to resources, such as file shares and websites, is simple for all the users in a forest, regardless of the domain they belong to.

From a replication-boundaries perspective, only configuration and schema partitions from the AD DS database will be replicated to all domains in forest. Because of this, if you want to implement applications with incompatible schemas, you need to deploy additional forests. The global catalog is also *part* of replication boundaries. This makes it easy to search for AD DS objects from other domains in the forest.

Sites

The site is a logical representative of AD DS objects, such as computers and services, that are specific to a physical location. In a multisite environment, site implementation provides a better authentication process.

Organizational Units

An **Organizational Unit (OU)** is a logical object in AD DS for collecting users, groups, and computers. You can use OUs to consolidate users, computers, groups, and other objects for simplified management using GPOs linking, or to delegate administrative rights. You can also use OUs to represent a hierarchical and logical structure inside the organization domain. Although no specific rule exists for a logical OU structure, you can create OUs to represent departments in an organization, geographical regions, or anything else based on your organization needs.

If you want to organize the hierarchical and logical structure of your organization, it isn't recommended to add more than five levels of OUs nesting. Although there's no limit for the nesting of OUs, the Distinguished Names can become very long, which could cause problems for some applications.

Containers

A container is an object that provides an organizational framework for use in AD DS. Most containers are created by default. The biggest difference between a container and an OU is that containers don't have the ability to link to GPOs.

Physical components

The physical components are just as important as the logical components. These will be described in the following sections.

Domain controllers

The domain controller is the most important physical component of AD DS. Each domain controller contains a copy of the AD DS database and the SYSVOL folder. The domain controller uses multi-master replication to copy changed data from one domain controller to an other. As a replication mechanism, Windows Server 2016 can only use **Distributed File Systems (DFS)**. The **File Replication Service (FRS)**, which was used in earlier versions of Windows Server, was deprecated in Windows Server 2016.

Domain controllers host the Kerberos authentication service, which is used when a user or a computer account needs to sign in to the domain. The **Key Distribution Center (KDC)** issues the **ticket-granting ticket (TGT)** to the account that's signing in to the AD DS domain. Each domain controller can host a copy of the global catalog.

It's highly recommended that each domain has at least two domain controllers for availability purposes.

Read-only domain controllers

The read-only domain controller is a read-only installation of AD DS. By design, RODCs are ideal for branch offices that don't have appropriate physical security or dedicated IT support. By default, RODC doesn't cache any user passwords, but that's configurable.

Data stores

The data store is an AD DS database that's stored in `C:\Windows\NTDS\ntds.dit`. Each domain controller in the domain stores a copy of the AD DS database and all the related associated log files.

Global catalogs

The global catalog is a partial read-only copy of all objects in the forest. The purpose of the global catalog is to speed up searching for objects stored on different domains in the forest. Within a single domain, each query for objects is sent directly to the domain controllers in that domain, but if you want to include results from other domains in the forest, the query needs to be sent to the global catalog server. The global catalog server is the domain controller that hosts the global catalog, which, by default, is the first deployed domain controller in the forest root domain. The global catalog maintains the subset of attributes that are useful in cross-domain searches, such as `givenName`, `displayName`, and the mail.

It's highly recommended that the global catalog server and the infrastructure FSMO role are on separate servers. The infrastructure master communicates regularly with the global catalog server in order to keep cross-domain references up to date. When the infrastructure master detects that a cross-domain reference is out of date, it obtains the updated data from the global catalog server and replicates that to other DCs in its own domain. This process works well, but only in cases where the global catalog and the infrastructure master aren't on the same server.

You can find more information at `https://support.microsoft.com/en-us/help/248047/phantoms-tombstones-and-the-infrastructure-master`.

What's new in AD DS in Windows Server 2016

Like every new Windows Server version, Windows Server 2016 comes with several new features as part of AD DS:

- **Privileged Access Management (PAM)**: This allows you to separate the permissions required for specific administrative tasks. With PAM implemented, the user needs to request permission to perform some specific tasks, instead of having permanent access or a membership with granted access. PAM is based on the Microsoft Identity Manager.

- **Azure Active Directory Join (Azure AD Join)**: With Azure AD Join, you are now able to join on-premises devices to Azure AD and improve the management of cloud-only and hybrid environments. Azure AD Join allows you to join devices directly to the cloud, without having on-premise AD DS. For devices that are joined directly to the cloud, some MDM solutions need to be used for device management.
- **Microsoft Passport**: Microsoft Passport is one of the new AD DS features supported in Windows Server 2016. Microsoft Passport provides a certificate-based authentication against on-premise AD DS and Azure AD that can replace the use of passwords.

AD DS administration tools

AD DS management is one of the most common daily tasks for administrators. There are a few different options to manage AD DS environments. You can sign in to the domain controller directly, you can manage AD DS through RDS, you can use RSAT from your domain-joined computer, you can use Server Manager for Remote Management, or you can use PowerShell remoting.

If you decide to use the GUI, several tools and Microsoft Management Consoles (MMC) are included by default in Windows Server 2016:

- **Active Directory Administrative Center**: This GUI tool is natively Windows PowerShell-based. The improved functionalities of this management tool give you the ability to perform almost all known Active Directory tasks. The Active Directory Administrative Center can be installed on Windows Server 2008 R2 servers or later and Windows 7 or later operating systems. With Active Directory Administrative Center, you can perform the following actions:
    - Create and manage users, computers, and groups
    - Create and manage OUs
    - Manage multiple domains within a single instance of the Active Directory Administrative Center
    - Search and filter AD DS data
    - Configure fine-grained password policies
    - Recover objects from the Active Directory Recycle Bin
- **Active Directory Users and Computers**: An MMC snap-in that gives you the ability to manage most common tasks and resources, including users, groups, and computers.

- **Active Directory Sites and Services**: An MMC snap-in that manages replication, network topology, and other site-related services.
- **Active Directory Domains and Trusts**: An MMC snap-in that configures and maintains trust relationships between domains and forests.
- **Active Directory Schema**: An MMC snap-in that modifies the definitions of AD DS attributes and object classes.
- **Active Directory module for Windows PowerShell**: Supports AD DS administration. This is one of the most important management components.

Although many administrators are familiar with Active Directory Users and Computers, the Active Directory Administrative Center replaces it and provides many more capabilities.

By default, the Active Directory Schema snap-in isn't fully installed. In order to enable the Schema snap-in, you need to start Command Prompt as an Administrator and run the `regsvr32 schmmgmt.dll` command.

Installing and configuring the Active Directory

The process of configuring the Active Directory starts by installing the Active Directory Domain Services role on Windows Server 2016. Once you've done this, you'll have installed the AD DS role, but AD DS will not yet be configured on the server. During configuration, you need to answer a few questions in order to successfully deploy a new forest or an additional domain controller.

Installing a new forest and domain controller

Before, or during, the configuration of a new forest or an additional domain controller, you need to answer the following questions:

- Do you want to install a new forest, a new tree, or an additional domain controller?
- What is the FQDN of the domain?
- Which domain and forest functional level do you need?
- Do you want to install DNS on the domain controller?

- Does the domain controller host the global catalog?
- Do you want to install RODC?
- What will the **Directory Service Restore Mode (DSRM)** password be?
- What is the name of NetBIOS?
- Where will the AD DS database, logs, and SYSVOL be stored?

Once you have the answers to these questions, you can start by configuring new forests or additional domain controllers. The whole process can be done through a GUI wizard or PowerShell. Both approaches will be covered in this chapter.

 In the following examples, I'll show you how to create a new forest, **mcsacertguide.local**, with the highest domain and forest functional level and with the default location for the AD DS database, logs, and SYSVOL folder.

Installing a new forest (GUI)

Configuring a new forest using the GUI wizard is a straightforward process. If you have the answers to all the questions listed previously, you just need to follow the wizard:

1. Go to **Deployment Configuration**:
    1. Select **Add a new forest**.
    2. Enter a **Root domain name**.
2. Go to **Domain Controller Options**:
    1. Select Forest and Domain functional level.
    2. Check **Domain Name System (DNS) server**.
    3. Type the DSRM password.
3. Go to **Additional Options** and verify the NetBIOS name, or change it if you need to.
4. Go to **Paths** and change the paths if necessary. Otherwise, you can skip this step and keep the default values.
5. Go to **Review Options**. Once you have configured everything, you need to review the configuration and confirm it.
6. Go to **Prerequisites Check**. If you pass all the prerequisite checks, you just need to click Install and wait for AD DS to install.
7. After the installation of AD DS, the server will restart automatically.

Installing a new forest on a Server Core installation

If you want to install and configure AD DS on Server Core, you need to use PowerShell instead of the GUI wizard. The steps in the process are same, but the approach is different:

1. To begin with, you need to install an AD DS role on the server using the following command:

   ```
   Install-WindowsFeature AD-Domain-Services -IncludeAllSubFeature -
   IncludeManagementTools
   ```

   In the `Install-WindowsFeature` cmdlet, the `-IncludeAllSubFeatures` and `-IncludeManagementTolls` switches are very important. In this case, without those switches, Group Policy Management and RSAT for AD DS and AD LDS won't be installed.

2. Once you have successfully installed the Active Directory Domain Services role, you need to run the following commands:

   ```
   Import-Module ADDSDeployment
   Install-ADDSForest -DomainName "mcsacertguide.local" -
   CreateDnsDelegation:$false -ForestMode "WinThreshold" -DomainMode
   "WinThreshold" -DomainNetbiosName "MCSACERTGUIDE" -InstallDns:$true
   -DatabasePath "C:\Windows\NTDS" -LogPath "C:\Windows\NTDS" -
   SysvolPath "C:\Windows\SYSVOL" -NoRebootOnCompletion:$false -
   Force:$true
   ```

   The `WinThreshold` parameter in the `-DomainMode` and `-ForestMode` PowerShell switches defines that the highest domain and forest functional level will be used.

   The switch for the DSRM password isn't included in this command, but once you run it, you will be asked to enter and confirm the password.

Installing a domain controller from Install from Media (IFM)

Sometimes, the network connection between two sites can be slow or unreliable. Bad network connectivity can cause issues with user authentication and reduce productivity. In this case, the best solution is to deploy an additional domain controller to the secondary site. The domain controller on the site will improve the authentication process, but before you add an additional domain controller to the domain, you need to avoid bad network issues during the initial AD DS replication, because the complete AD DS database and SYSVOL folder need to be replicated to the additional domain controller. Using the **Install from Media (IFM)** option, you will significantly reduce the amount of network traffic during the initial replication. To install the domain controller by IFM, you basically need to create a backup of AD DS and save the data to a USB drive or shared location.

The process starts on a read-write domain controller. RODC isn't a candidate for IFM, because you can't perform AD DS backup on a read-only database. You need to use the ndtsutil command-line tools to create an AD DS backup, which will be used later to promote an additional domain controller:

```
Ntdsutil
Activate instance ntds
Ifm
create SYSVOL full C:\IFM
```

The whole process will last less than one minute, and then you can find all the necessary files in the provided folder. Once you have the AD DS backup on a local drive, you need to copy all the files to a new domain controller using a USB or external drive. The process of promoting a new domain controller using IFM is the same as the standard way, with only one difference. If you use the GUI wizard, on the **Additional Setting** tab, you just need to check the **Install from Media** checkbox and browse to the local folder where the AD DS backup files are stored.

The files will be verified automatically. If everything is fine with the AD DS backup, you will be able to go on to the next tab:

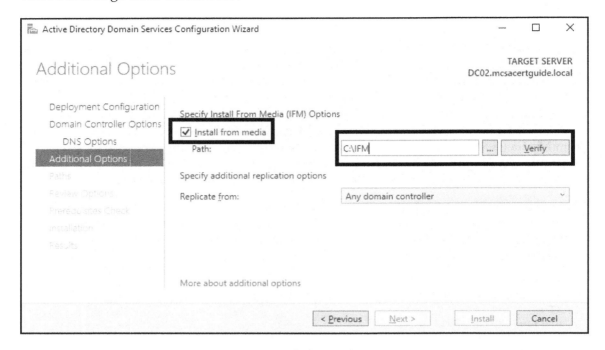

If the path isn't correct, you'll receive an error message:

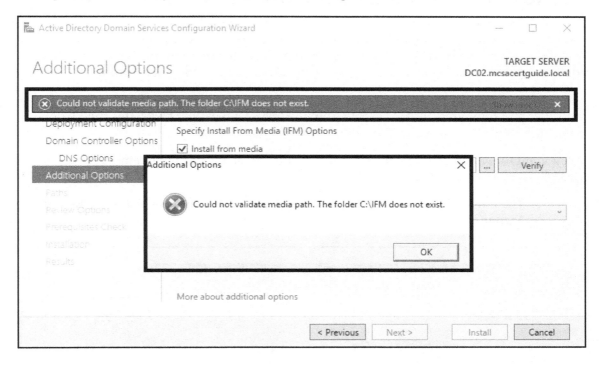

If you use PowerShell to promote a new domain controller, you just need to add one more switch in the PowerShell command. You need to add a few more switches, so the command will look as follows:

```
Import-Module ADDSDeployment
Install-ADDSDomainController -DomainName "mcsacertguide.local" -
CriticalReplicationOnly:$false -InstallationMediaPath "C:\IFM" -
CreateDnsDelegation:$false -ForestMode "WinThreshold" -DomainMode
"WinThreshold" -DomainNetbiosName "MCSACERTGUIDE" -InstallDns:$true -
SiteName "Default-First-Site-Name" -DatabasePath "C:\Windows\NTDS" -LogPath
"C:\Windows\NTDS" -SysvolPath "C:\Windows\SYSVOL" -
NoRebootOnCompletion:$false -Force:$true
```

After initial replication using IFM, the new domain controller will replicate the other domain controllers using multi-master replication, the standard replication method.

Removing a domain controller from a domain

Adding a new domain controller was covered in the previous section. We now know how to deploy a new forest or an additional domain controller with the GUI wizard or with PowerShell commands. Sometimes, you need to remove the domain controller from the domain, a process that's logically different from adding a new domain controller.

The domain controller removal process consists of two steps: demoting the domain controller and removing an AD DS role from the server. Like other tasks, this can be done using either the GUI wizard or PowerShell commands.

If you want to remove the domain controller using the GUI wizard, the removal process consists of several steps that need to be performed:

1. The removal process starts with **Remove Roles and Features** using the **Server Manager** console:

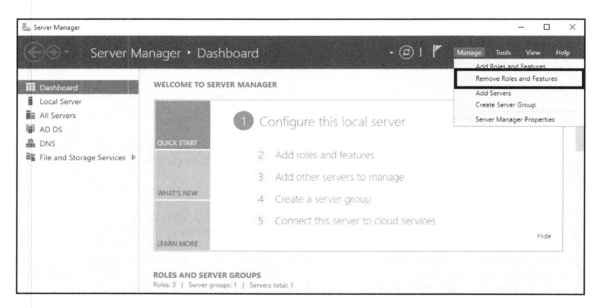

2. You need to select the **Active Directory Domain Services** role, as that role needs to be removed:

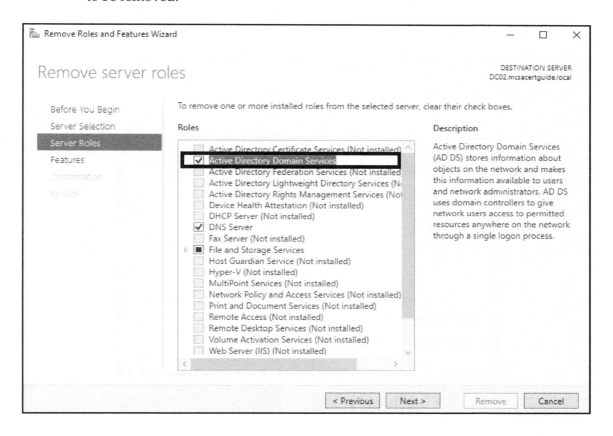

3. Because the removal process is dependent on the demotion of the domain controller, the process will fail on validation. The wizard will give you the option to click on **Demote this domain controller**, as shown in the following screenshot. A new wizard for the demotion process will be opened automatically:

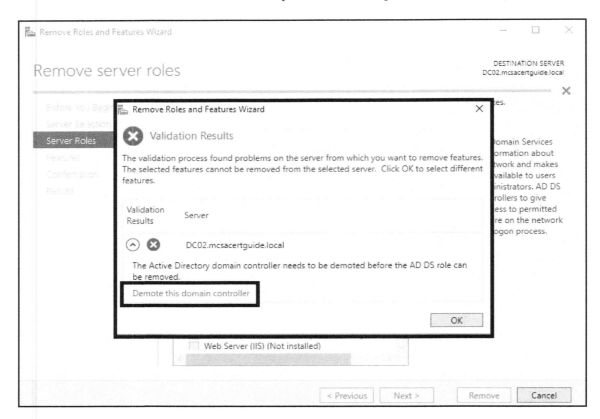

4. If your domain controller is not the last in the domain, you don't need to check the **Force the removal of this domain controller** checkbox. If your domain controller is the last in the domain, or if it doesn't have any connectivity to other domain controllers, then you do need to check this checkbox:

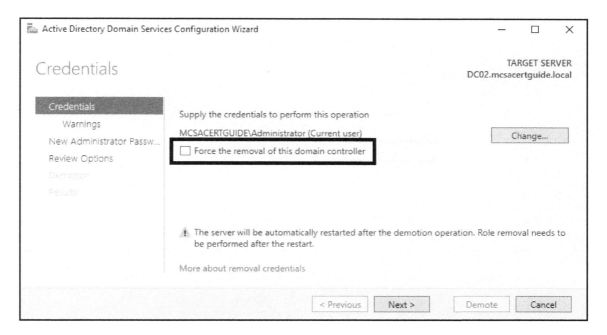

5. Confirm that you want to proceed with the domain controller removal:

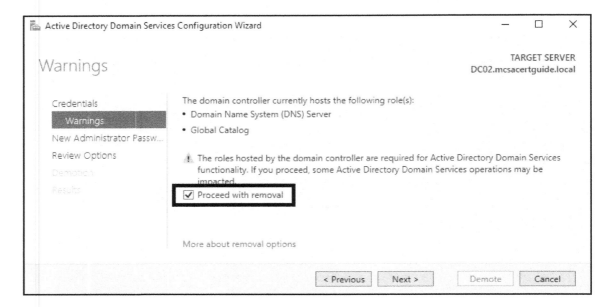

6. Finally, you need to click on the **Demote** button to start the demotion process:

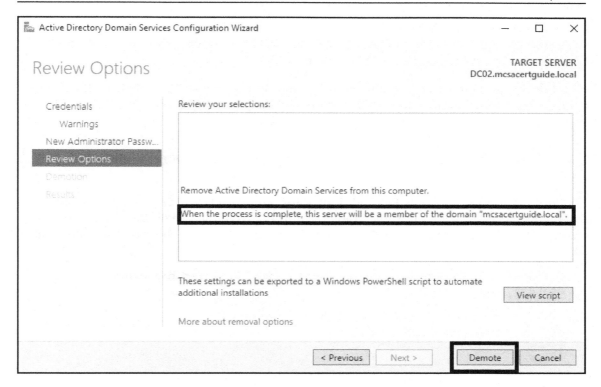

On the very first tab of the GUI wizard to demote the domain controller, you'll have the option to select the **Force the removal of this domain controller** checkbox. Don't check this checkbox unless the domain controller isn't the last domain controller in the domain. If you check this, the demoting process will not inform other domain controllers about the change, and the metadata cleanup process will need to be performed manually.

During the process, you'll be asked to enter your password twice. That is because the domain controller doesn't have local users or groups, and if you demote the domain controller from the server, the server will stay part of the domain as a member server. This means that the local users and groups will be active on the server again. The provided password is for the local Administrator account.

Once the domain controller is successfully demoted from the server, the server will restart. After the server is restarted, you need to start the AD DS removal process from the Server Manager in order to remove the AD DS role from the server.

If you decide to demote the domain controller and remove the AD DS role from the server using PowerShell, you need to start the process by demoting the domain controller. After that, you can remove the AD DS role from the server:

```
Import-Module ADDSDeployment
Uninstall-ADDSDomainController -DemoteOperationMasterRole:$true -
Force:$true
```

You'll be asked to enter a new local administrator password twice. Once the PowerShell command successfully demotes the domain controller from the server, the server will restart. After the server is restarted, you need to run the following command to remove an AD DS role from the server:

```
Uninstall-WindowsFeature AD-Domain-Services -IncludeManagementTools -
Restart
```

 If you try to remove AD DS before demoting the domain controller, PowerShell will return an error.

Upgrading a domain controller

Upgrading a domain controller is a process that's the same for all versions of Windows Server operating systems from Windows Server 2008. You can do this in one of two ways:

- Upgrade the operating system on existing domain controllers in place.
- Carry out a clean install and migrate to Windows Server 2016 as a new domain controller in the domain.

I personally prefer the second method, because when you finish, you will have a clean installation. The DNS records and AD DS database will be replicated on a new server.

If you want to upgrade the domain and the forest functional level in the running domain to Windows Server 2016, all your domain controllers must be Windows Server 2016.

In-place upgrade

If you want to upgrade an existing domain controller to Windows Server 2016, you need to perform an in-place upgrade. The source domain controller needs to be Windows Server 2008 or later. The in-place upgrade process doesn't perform an automatic schema and domain update; you need to run those command-line commands manually. The installation media includes the `adprep.exe` tool in `\Support\Adprep`. You need to run the following commands:

```
adprep.exe /forestprep
adprep.exe /domainprep
```

Once you have successfully performed the `adprep` commands, you can start by installing the upgraded operating system on a domain controller with the older OS version.

When you promote a server running Windows Server 2016 to be a domain controller in an existing domain and you have signed in as a member of the Schema Admins and Enterprise Admins groups, the AD DS schema automatically updates to Windows Server 2016.

Domain-controller migration

If you decide to avoid potential in-place upgrade issues, but still want to upgrade your domain controllers to Windows Server 2016, you need to perform domain-controller migration. Although the word *migration* might make you nervous, domain-controller migration is actually a straightforward process. You just need to have Windows Server 2016 as a clean, installed operating system. Then, you can start the process of adding additional domain controllers in an existing domain, which is explained in one of the previous sections. During this process, DNS Zones, AD DS databases, and SYSVOL folders will be replicated on the new server.

Once you have at least two Windows Server 2016 domain controllers added to the existing domain, you can start the process of removing the old domain controllers. Before doing this, however, you need to do the following:

- Transfer all FSMO roles to new domain controllers.
- Change the IP addresses for the DNS servers to all domain computers.

Once you finish those tasks, you can start to remove the old domain controllers from the domain. When you remove the old domain controllers, you can upgrade the domain and the forest functional level to Windows Server 2016. After that, the domain and domain controllers are fully upgraded to the Windows Server 2016 version.

Transferring FSMO roles will be explained in a later section of this chapter.

Configuring a global catalog server

As we've mentioned, the global catalog server is a domain controller that holds a global catalog. By default, the first domain controller in the forest root domain is the global catalog server. If you have a multi-domain environment that needs to be more scalable for cross-forest queries, you need to implement more than one global catalog server.

As mentioned in an earlier section, the global catalog server shouldn't be a domain controller that holds the Infrastructure FSMO role.

Configuring the global catalog on the domain controller can be done using the Active Directory Sites and Services MMC Snap-in or PowerShell commands. If you want to do this using a GUI, you just need to open the properties of domain controller and check the global catalog checkbox:

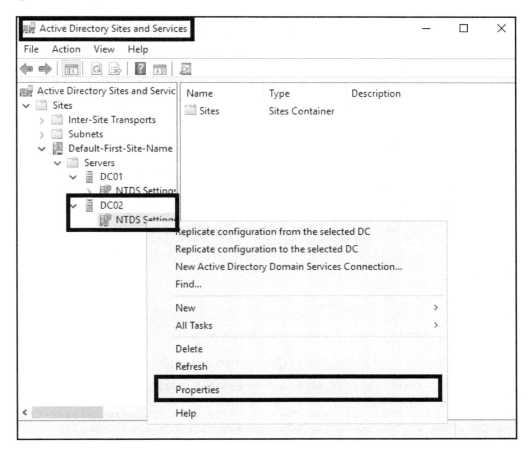

Once you open NTDS properties, you will be able to promote the server to a Global Catalog server and also remove the Global Catalog role from the server:

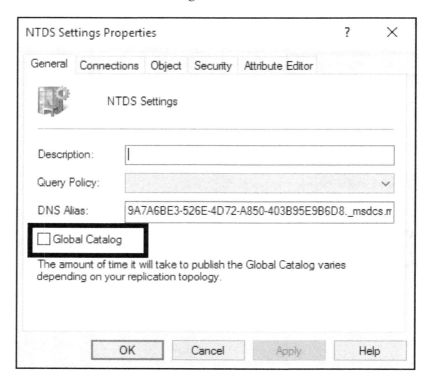

Using PowerShell, you need to run one of the following commands:

```
Set-ADObject -Identity (Get-ADDomainController DC02).ntdssettingsobjectdn -
Replace @{options='1'}
Set-ADObject "CN=NTDS Settings,CN=DC02,CN=Servers,CN=Default-First-Site-
Name,CN=Sites,CN=Configuration,DC=mcsacertguide,DC=local" -Replace
@{options='1'}
```

Transferring and seizing operation master roles

Every forest and domain has FSMO roles that are important for a properly functioning AD DS environment. In some scenarios, such as a single domain infrastructure, the first domain controller in the forest root domain will hold all FSMO roles. Statistically, most organizations have this FSMO structure. Sometimes, however, you need to move one or more FSMO roles to another domain controller. This process can be planned, if we are demoting old domain controllers or workload balancing, or unplanned, due to a hardware failure of the domain controller that holds FSMO roles.

Transferring FSMO roles

Transferring an FSMO role is a planned action, in most cases, because we are demoting old domain controllers. When you transfer a role, the latest data will replicate to the target server. To transfer an FSMO role using the GUI, you need to use the following AD MMC Snap-ins:

MMC Snap-in	FSMO role
Active Directory Users and Computers	PDC emulator, Infrastructure master, RID master
Active Directory Domain and Trust	Domain-naming master
Active Directory Schema	Schema master

To transfer the PDC Emulator, Infrastructure master, and RID master FSMO roles, you need to use the Active Directory Users and Computers MMC Snap-in:

1. Open MMC Snap-in.
2. Select the domain and right-click on it.
3. Select **Operation Masters**.

You will see three different tabs, one for each of these FSMO roles, and you can then perform a transfer.

To transfer the Domain-naming master FSMO role, you need to use the Active Directory Domain and Trust MMC Snap-in:

1. Open MMC Snap-in.
2. Select **Active Directory Domains and Trusts** and right-click on it.
3. Select **Operation Masters**.

Then you will be able to perform the FSMO role transfer.

To transfer the Schema master FSMO role, you need to use a customized MMC Snap-in:

1. If you haven't done so already, register the schema by running the `regsvr32 schmmgmt.dll` command.
2. Open MMC Snap-in and open Active Directory Schema.
3. Select the **Active Directory Schema** and right-click on it.
4. Select **Operation Masters**.

Then you will be able to perform the FSMO role transfer.

Of course, the FSMO role transfer can also be done using PowerShell commands:

```
Move-ADDirectoryServerOperationMasterRole -Identity TargetDCName -
OperationMasterRole FSMORoleName
```

In one command, you can move more than one role. Role names need to be separated with commas.

As a parameter for the `-OperationMasterRole` switch in the PowerShell command, numbers can also be used instead of names. Here is a list of the roles and their corresponding numbers:

- PDCEmulator = 0
- RIDMaster = 1
- InfrastructureMaster = 2
- SchemaMaster = 3
- DomainNamingMaster = 4

Seizing FSMO roles

FSMO role-seizing is a last-resort action and is only used in scenarios in which the original domain controller isn't available, due to a hardware failure or accidental deletion. The available data on the other domain controllers might be incomplete or out of date. Unlike transferring, FSMO role-seizing can't be performed using Active Directory MMC Snap-ins. FSMO role-seizing can be completed only using PowerShell or the `ntdsutil` command-line tool.

The PowerShell command for FSMO role-seizing is the same as for transferring, but we need to include the `-Force` switch:

```
Move-ADDirectoryServerOperationMasterRole -Identity TargetDCName -
OperationMasterRole FSMORoleName -Force
```

 To find out more about how to transfer or seize FSMO roles using ntdsutil, check out https://support.microsoft.com/en-gb/help/ 255504/using-ntdsutil-exe-to-transfer-or-seize-fsmo-roles-to-a-domain-control.

Installing and configuring a read-only domain controller (RODC)

As mentioned earlier, RODC is a read-only installation of AD DS. RODC installation can be performed in two different ways: a standard domain controller installation using the GUI wizard or PowerShell, or by creating a pre-staged computer account in AD DS for RODC. Both approaches will give you same result, but the pre-staged account configuration will force you to configure more settings related to RODC before promoting the server to RODC.

If you decide to go with the easier approach of using the GUI wizard, you just need to check the **Read only domain controller (RODC)** checkbox on the Domain Controller Options page:

1. Go to **Deployment Configuration** and select **Add a new domain to existing forest**.
2. Go to **Domain Controller Options**:
    1. Select the Forest and Domain functional level.
    2. Check **Domain Name System (DNS) server**.
    3. Check **Read only domain controller (RODC)**.
    4. Type the DSRM password.
3. Go to **RODC Options**:
    1. Define the RODC Administrator account (optional).
    2. Define which users or groups can replicate their passwords to RODC.
4. Go to **Additional Options** and verify the NetBIOS name, or change it if you need to.

5. Go to **Paths** and change the path if necessary. Otherwise, you can skip this step and keep the default values.
6. Go to **Review Options**. Once you have configured everything, you need to review the configuration and confirm it.
7. Go to **Prerequisites Check**. If you pass all prerequisite checks, you just need to click Install and wait for AD DS to install.
8. After the installation of AD DS on the RODC, the server will restart automatically.

The PowerShell command that you will use to install RODC has a few more switches than the command that we used to install a standard domain controller:

```
Import-Module ADDSDeployment
Install-ADDSDomainController -DomainName "mcsacertguide.local" -
InstallDns:$true -ReadOnlyReplica:$true -NoGlobalCatalog:$false -
CriticalReplicationOnly:$false -AllowPasswordReplicationAccountName
@("MCSACERTGUIDE\Allowed RODC Password Replication Group") -
DenyPasswordReplicationAccountName @("BUILTIN\Administrators",
"BUILTIN\Server Operators", "BUILTIN\Backup Operators", "BUILTIN\Account
Operators", "MCSACERTGUIDE\Denied RODC Password Replication Group") -
SiteName "Default-First-Site-Name" -DatabasePath "C:\Windows\NTDS" -LogPath
"C:\Windows\NTDS" -SysvolPath "C:\Windows\SYSVOL" -
NoRebootOnCompletion:$false -Force:$true
```

By default, RODC doesn't cache any passwords, for security reasons. In the RODC environment, you need to determine which passwords will be cached on RODC and which accounts need to be authenticated on a writable domain controller. By default, in the RODC environment, the system creates a domain-wide password-replication policy with two security groups:

- **Allowed RODC Password Replication Group**: Members of this group are allowed to cache passwords in RODC. By default, this group doesn't have any members.
- **Denied RODC Password Replication Group**: Members of this group aren't allowed to cache passwords in RODC. Some security-critical groups are members of this group by default, such as Administrators, Server Operators, Backup Operators, and Account Operators.

Configuring domain controller cloning

From Windows Server 2012, the fastest way to deploy a new domain controller is to clone computers. Prior to Windows Server 2012, only domain members could be cloned. Cloning copies the virtual drive of VMs and changes some configuration parameters, such as the IP address and the computer name. Cloning provides some benefits, such as rapidly provisioning computers with the same configuration and provisioning test environments.

Successful domain controller cloning requires the following:

- Hyper-V on Windows Server 2012 or later.
- Virtualized domain controllers that need to be Windows Server 2012 or later.
- A PDC emulator that runs on Windows Server 2012 or later. The PDC emulator must be online when the virtual domain controller clones start for the first time.

The domain-controller cloning process consist of several steps:

1. Add the source domain controller to the **Cloneable Domain Controllers** group.
2. Verify that the apps and services on the source domain support cloning and generate an XML file using the following PowerShell command:

   ```
   Get-ADDCCloningExcludedApplicationList
   Get-ADDCCloningExcludedApplicationList -GenerateXML
   ```

3. Create the `DCCloneConfig.xml` file. When the cloning process recognizes it, a new domain controller will be created from the clone:

   ```
   New-ADDCCloneConfigFile
   ```

4. Shut down the source domain controller and export the virtual machine.
5. Import a new virtual machine using the exported files.
6. Name the new virtual machine and then copy the virtual machine (create a new unique ID).
7. Start the cloned virtual machine.

Once you start the cloned domain controller, the clone checks whether the virtual machine identifier exists and reads the information stored in the previously created `DCCloneConfig.xml` file.

The `DCCloneConfig.xml` file can be created with default values or with customized values using the `New-ADDCCloneConfigFile` PowerShell command. For more information, visit `https://docs.microsoft.com/en-us/powershell/module/addsadministration/new-addccloneconfigfile`.

Active Directory users and computers

Although AD DS has a lot of object types, its users, groups, and computers are the most important. These accounts are directly related to users and their computers, and to the server infrastructure. In this section, we'll explain how you can create user and computer accounts. Group management will be covered in the next section of this chapter.

Creating and managing users accounts

Each user object in AD DS has more than a few attributes that can be configured. We can't cover all user object attributes here, but the most important attributes related to identity will be covered in this section.

All user accounts can be created using a few different GUI or command-line tools. For administrators who like to use GUI tools, there are two different MMC Snap-ins: Active Directory Administrative Center and Active Directory Users and Computers.

The Active Directory Administrative Center is important for this certification. It has a lot of improvements compared to Active Directory Users and Computers, and exam questions are focused on this MMC Snap-in.

For command-line-oriented administrators, the PowerShell and Dsadd command-line tools are valuable options.

To prepare for the exam, your focus needs to be on PowerShell, but some questions might be related to the Dsadd command-line tool. All examples in this section will present PowerShell commands.

Creating a user using GUI tools is a straightforward process, but it's different depending on which MMC Snap-in you decide to use. With Active Directory Users and Computers, creating a user requires only the most important attributes that need to be configured:

- First name
- Last name
- User login name
- Password

With this information in the user account, the user will be able to log in to the domain-joined machine. All other attributes, such as group membership, company name, and phone number, must be configured later if you use Active Directory Users and Computers. However, if you decide to use the Active Directory Administrative Center for user creation, the process will be a little bit different. You need to add all the attributes that were necessary when using Active Directory Users and Computers, but all other attributes can be added at the same time during the creation process.

The creation process using PowerShell can include several commands in a row. Depending on which switches are used in the PowerShell cmdlet, different attributes can be included. The following example shows you the command for user creation using PowerShell with the same parameters used in previous examples for GUI MMC Snap-ins:

```
New-ADUser -GivenName Vladimir -Surname Stefanovic -Name "Vladimir
Stefanovic" -UserPrincipalName vladimir.stefanovic@mcsacertguide.local -
SamAccountName vladimir.stefanovic -AccountPassword (Read-Host
-AsSecureString "Enter password") -Enabled $true
```

 Once a user account is created with PowerShell, it will not be enabled unless you include the -Enabled with parameter $true switch. If you forget to add that switch to the command, you can enable the account later using the PowerShell Enable-ADAccount cmdlet.

If, for any reason, you want to copy a user account, only Active Directory Users and Computers can offer this; the Active Directory Administrative Center doesn't have this option. With PowerShell, you can do this by creating scripts or creating a user from a template:

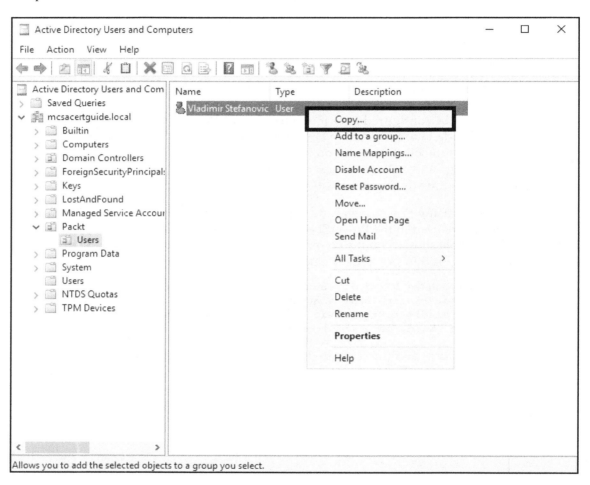

Only the most commonly used attributes are copied to the new user account:

- Group memberships
- Home directories
- Profile settings
- Logon scripts
- Logon hours
- Password settings
- Department name
- Manager

Once you create a user account, using any of the provided methods, the account will be fully operational and other users will be able to use them. If you want to change some of the attributes, which is one of the most common tasks for user accounts, this can also be done using the same MMC Snap-ins or PowerShell. If you want to use the GUI MMC Snap-in, you just need to go to the properties for the selected account and change the value of the specific attributes. The `Set-ADUser` PowerShell cmdlet needs to be used if you want to change the attributes, and you can add more than one switch in a PowerShell command:

```
Set-ADUser -Identity vladimir.stefanovic -Company "Packt" -Department "IT"
```

Deleting a user account can also be done using management tools, MMC Snap-ins, or PowerShell. In both MMC Snap-ins, you just need to right-click on the user account and select **Delete**. PowerShell for AD DS has the `Remove-ADUser` cmdlet. The following command will delete the user account without any additional questions:

```
Remove-ADUser -Identity vladimir.stefanovic -Confirm:$false
```

If you don't use `-Confirm:$False`, you'll be asked to confirm the deletion of the user account.

By default, the user account isn't protected from accidental deletion. That attribute is unchecked by design, and if you want to enable it, you need to make some changes to the user account. Protecting the user account from accidental deletion is very important, because once deleted account will prevent the user to log on to the system and access to corporate resources. The easiest way to do this using a GUI MMC Snap-in is to use the Active Directory Administrative Center. You just need to check the **Protect from accidental deletion** checkbox. Using this MMC Snap-in, you can configure this protection during the creation of your user account:

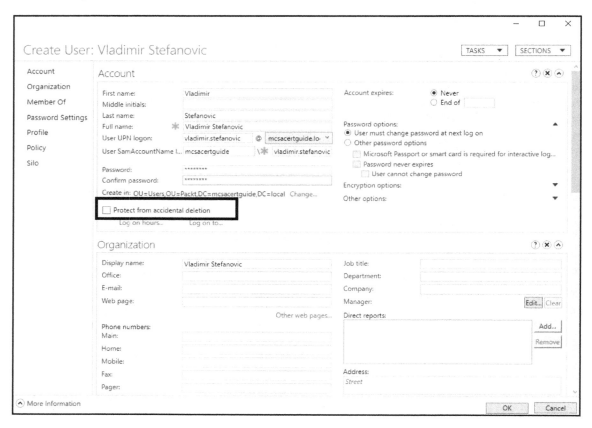

If you want to use the MMC Snap-in Active Directory Users and Computers, you need to edit the properties of the user account on the **Object** Tab, and check the **Protect object from accidental deletion** checkbox:

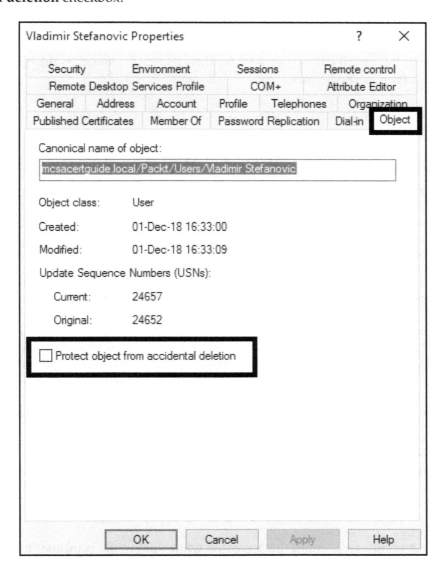

The PowerShell cmdlet for this task is `Set-ADObject`. This needs to be started once the user account is created:

```
Set-ADObject -Identity:"CN=Vladimir
Stefanovic,OU=Users,OU=Packt,DC=mcsacertguide,DC=local"-
ProtectedFromAccidentalDeletion:$true
```

In this cmdlet, the parameter for the `-Identity` switch is the object's Distinguished Name.

Creating and managing computer accounts

Computers, like users, are security principals in AD DS that have an account with a logon name and password. Unlike users, the password for computer accounts is managed by Windows Server and changes automatically on a periodic basis. Computer accounts also authenticate against the domain and belong to one or more groups in AD DS. The most common tasks for computer accounts are moving between OUs and configuring properties.

Although computer accounts are automatically created when joining a computer to a domain, the proper procedure for this task requires us to create a computer account manually in AD DS before joining the computer to the domain. The creation process is very similar to creating a user account, and like a user account, it can be done using either MMC Snap-ins or PowerShell. Using Active Directory Users and Computers, you just need to populate the Computer Name field, and all other attributes can be configured later. Using the Active Directory Administrative Center, you need to populate the **Computer Name** field, because that's mandatory, but you'll configure many other attributes as well. PowerShell lovers will use the following command to create a computer account:

```
New-ADComputer -Name Server03 -Path
"OU=Computers,OU=Packt,DC=mcsacertguide,DC=local"
```

By default, all computer accounts that are created using the New-ADComputer PowerShell cmdlet and without the `-Path` switch will be stored in the `Computers` system container.

A computer account that's created while joining the computer to the domain will be stored in the `Computers` system container as well.

All management tasks on a computer account can be done using either MMC Snap-ins or PowerShell. If you want to use MMC Snap-ins, you just need to configure some properties of the computer account. If you want to make changes using PowerShell, however, you need to use the `Set-ADComputer` or `Set-ADObject` PowerShell cmdlets, depending on the attribute that needs to be changed. Like user accounts, computer accounts are not by default protected from accidental deletion. During the creation process, this can be done using the Active Directory Administrative Center MMC Snap-in by checking the **Protect from accidental deletion** checkbox. This parameter can also be changed using Active Directory Users and Computers or the `Set-ADObject` PowerShell cmdlet using the same command, as for a user account:

```
Set-ADObject -Identity
"CN=Server03,OU=Computers,OU=Packt,DC=mcsacertguide,DC=local"-
ProtectedFromAccidentalDeletion:$true
```

Configuring templates

As mentioned earlier, only the Active Directory Users and Computers MMC Snap-in gives you the ability to copy a user account. With the new Active Directory Administrative Center MMC Snap-in or PowerShell, it isn't possible to copy a user account. However, from Windows Server 2012, you can create a user account with the most common parameters for a specific job role or department configured and use that account as a template. As mentioned earlier, attributes that are copied to the new user account are as follows:

- Group memberships
- Home directories
- Profile settings
- Logon scripts
- Logon hours
- Password settings
- Department name
- Manager

The template user account can be created using PowerShell or either of the MMC Snap-ins. Creating a new user account from the template can be done with the Active Directory Users and Computers MMC Snap-in with the copy option, as mentioned earlier, or using the PowerShell command:

```
$Template = Get-ADUser -Identity vladimir.stefanovic -Properties Company

New-ADUser -GivenName John -Surname Doe -Name "John Doe" -UserPrincipalName
john.doe@mcsacertguide.local -SamAccountName john.doe -AccountPassword
(Read-Host -AsSecureString "Enter password") -Enabled $true -Instance
$Template
```

Performing bulk Active Directory operations

The definition of a bulk operation is a single action that changes multiple objects. Performing a bulk operation is much faster than changing many objects individually. With any type of bulk operation, you need to be more accurate, because any typographic mistake will affect more than one object. The most common bulk operations are as follows:

- Creating new users from a CSV file
- Managing user attributes based on where they belong (OU, Department, Company, and so on)
- Disabling user accounts based on their activity

Although some bulk operations can be done using MMC Snap-ins, PowerShell is the most suitable tool to use. If you want to use PowerShell, you must understand the queries that will be used to list AD DS objects and how to work with .csv files. Then, you can create scripts that perform the bulk operations you need.

Using the **Get-ADUser** PowerShell cmdlet (for example), you can make a query to AD DS and list all user accounts. However, if you don't add a specific filter to your query, the result is likely to be useless. For this task, you need to understand the filtering parameters:

- **SearchBase**: Defines the AD DS path to begin searching.
- **SearchScope**: Defines at what level below the SearchBase the search should be performed.
- **ResultSetSize**: Defines how many objects to return in response to a query.
- **Properties**: Defines which object properties to return and display. To return all properties, type *.

All filtering of parameters, especially properties, can be made more precise using the following operators:

- -eq: Equal to
- -ne: Not equal to
- -lt: Less than
- -le: Less than or equal to
- -gt: Greater than
- -ge: Greater than or equal to
- -like: Uses wildcards for pattern matching

Once you make a correct query, you can use pipe (|) to perform another command to selected objects. For example, the following PowerShell command will configure the City attribute on all accounts that have the configured Department attribute with a value of IT:

```
Get-ADUser -Filter {Department -eq "IT"} | Set-ADUser -City London
```

Another suitable task for performing bulk operations is importing data from a CSV file. CSV files can contain more information than just lists and are often formatted as a spreadsheet. This approach is ideal if you need to create more than one user account at a time and the information populated in the file can be configured as an attribute in the user account. For example, the following is an example of a CSV file and the PowerShell script that will use the attribute from the CSV file:

```
Name,FirstName,LastName,UPN,SAM,Company

Vladimir Stefanovic,Vladimir,
Stefanovic,vladimir.stefanovic@mcsacertguide.local,vladimir.stefanovic,Pack
t

Sasha
Kranjac,Sasha,Kranjac,sasha.kranjac@mcsacertguide.local,sasha.kranjac,Packt

Import-Csv C:\Users.txt | foreach {New-ADUser -Name $_.Name -GivenName
$_.FirstName -Surname $_.LastName -UserPrincipalName $_.UPN -SamAccountName
$_.SAM -AccountPassword (Read-Host -AsSecureString Enter password) -Enabled
$true }
```

Implementing offline domain joins

Windows Server 2008 R2 introduced offline domain joins. This is a feature that allows you to join a computer to a domain without communicating directly with the domain controller. This works with client computers running Windows 7 or later or Windows Server 2008 R2 or later. To perform offline domain joins, you need to use the **djoin** command-line tool, which generates a domain-join file that will then be imported to the client computer. Offline domain join is useful, and mainly used, in scenarios where the machine that needs to be joined to the domain doesn't have network connectivity with domain controller or when you need to perform unattended installation of the Windows operating system.

To generate a djoin file, you need to run the following command and define parameters, such as a domain name, a computer name, and a location to save the offline domain join file to:

```
djoin.exe /provision /domain mcsacertguide.local /machine server01
/savefile c:\server01odj.txt
```

Once you create the offline domain join file, you need to copy the file to the desired computer and run the following command:

```
djoin.exe /requestODJ /loadfile c:\server01odj.txt /windowspath
%systemroot% /localos
```

Like a standard join to a domain, the computer needs to be restarted to complete the joining operation.

Managing accounts

For many different reasons, a user account might become inactive. If a user leaves a company for a certain period of time or resigns, and you think that the user doesn't need access to the account or the resources, the best practice is to disable a user account until you're sure it's safe to delete it. If you want to disable an account, you can use either of the MMC Snap-ins. All you need to do is select the desired user account and disable it by right-clicking and selecting **Disable** or **Disable Account**, depending on which MMC Snap-in you used. If you enable a user account, the procedure is same, but the options are different: **Enable** or **Enable Account**.

The PowerShell cmdlets that need to be used for this task are Enable-ADAccount and Disable-ADAccount, and the command needs to be as follows:

```
Disable-ADAccount -Identity vladimir.stefanovic
Enable-ADAccount -Identity vladimir.stefanovic
```

Active Directory groups and organizational units

In the previous section, we covered the management of user and computer accounts. You learned how to create and manage these types of accounts. In this section, we're going to look at the purpose of groups and organizational units.

In large enterprise networks, assigning permissions to user accounts is impractical. Adding users and computers to specific groups and then assigning permissions to resources is the only correct approach. It's important to understand group types and how to use them properly in order to manage access to resources or to assign management rights.

This section will also cover how to work with organizational units in AD DS.

Creating, configuring, and deleting groups

Like user and computer accounts, group accounts also need to be created. Once groups are created, they can be managed later. You can create groups using either of the MMC Snap-ins or PowerShell. You just need to know and define what group type and scope you need. Like all other objects covered in this chapter, Active Directory Users and Computers MMC Snap-in will give you the ability to create groups, but group configuration needs to be performed later, while the Active Directory Administrative Center MMC Snap-in allows you to configure more parameters at the same time.

If you decide to use Active Directory Users and Computers, you will see the following screen:

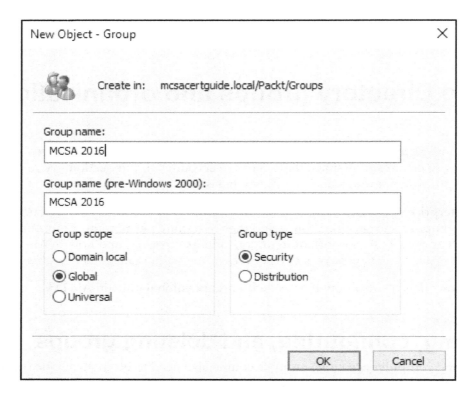

Active Directory Administrative Center is a little bit different. You will see the following screen:

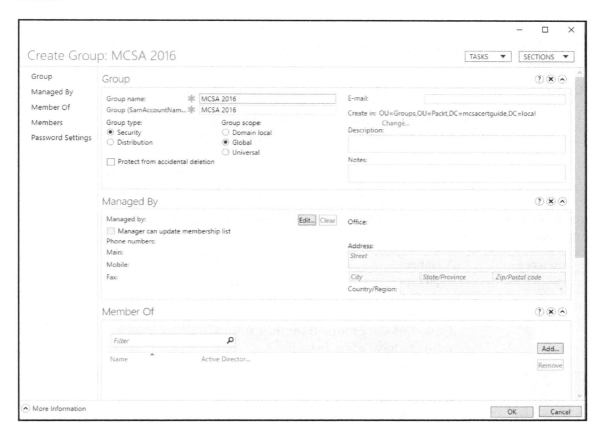

If you want to use PowerShell for group creation, you need to use the New–ADGroup cmdlet:

```
New-ADGroup -Name "MCSA 2016" -GroupCategory Security -GroupScope Global -
Path "OU=Packt,DC=mcsacertguide,DC=local"
```

Like user and computer accounts, group objects are not protected from accidental deletion by default. This needs to be configured, and the steps for MMC Snap-ins and PowerShell commands are the same as for user and computer accounts.

Configuring group nesting

Groups nesting is the process in which we add groups to other groups. This process creates a hierarchy of groups that can be helpful in supporting your roles and management rules. Microsoft recommends using IGDLA for group nesting, which is an acronym for the following:

(I) Identities **(G)** Global groups **(DL)** Domain-local groups **(A)** Access:

- **Identities (user and computer accounts)**: Members of global groups
- **Global groups represent specific business roles**: Members of domain-local groups
- **Domain-local groups**: Represent rules for access, such as Sales Read-Only
- **Access**: Resources in which domain-local groups have a specific type of access

In order to implement group nesting properly, knowing the scope of the group is important:

Group scope	Members	Assigned to
Local	Users, computers, global groups, and universal groups from any domain in the forest. Domain-local groups from the same domain, local users from the computer.	Local computer resources only
Domain-local	Users, computers, global groups, and universal groups from any domain in the forest. Domain-local groups from the same domain.	Local domain resources only
Global	Users, computers, and global groups from the same domain.	Any domain resource in the forest
Universal	Users, computers, global groups, and universal groups from any domain in the forest.	Any domain resource in the forest

Converting groups

The questions on how to convert groups are one of the trickiest in the MCSA exam.

Although changing the group scope looks like an easy process, in general, it's not.

The following list defines which group scope changes are allowed:

- **Global group to domain local group**: Not allowed directly. The global group first needs to be converted to a universal group. It can then be converted to a domain local group.
- **Global group to universal group**: Allowed only if the global group is not a member of another global group.
- **Domain local group to global group**: Not allowed directly. The domain local group first needs to be converted to a universal group. It can then be converted to a global group.
- **Domain local group to universal group**: Allowed only if the domain local group doesn't contain another domain local group.

In the following screenshot, you can see that the group scope is **Global**. If you want to change the group scope to **Domain local**, the option is grayed out and you can't do that. You can only convert the group to **Universal**:

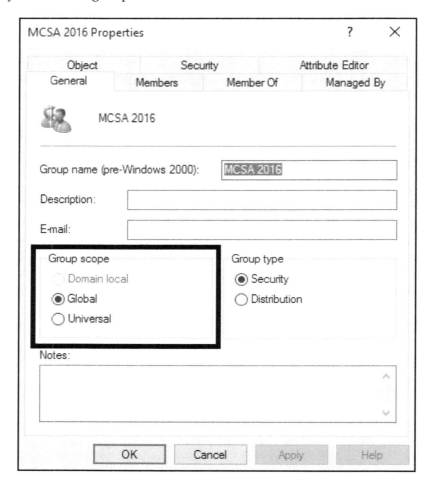

Once you have converted the group from **Global** to **Universal**, you will be able to convert the group to **Domain local**:

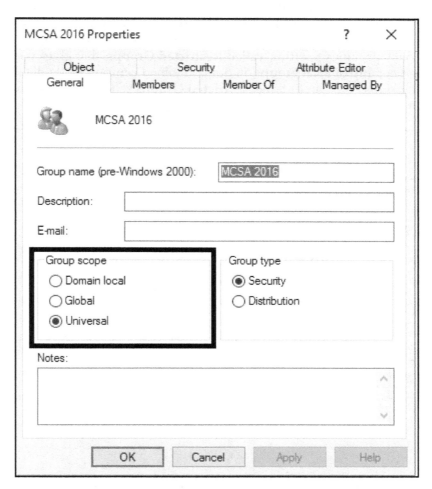

Managing group membership using Group Policy

Sometimes, managing group memberships can be time-consuming. For example, let's say you need to add a group to the local Administrators or the Account Operator group on all client computers in the domain. In this case, you need to use Group Policy to speed up the task. Group Policy provides a setting, called **Restricted Groups**, that gives you the ability to control the membership of local groups on domain-joined computers. By default, there are no configured groups. You can find the **Restricted Groups** setting by going to **Computer Configuration** | **Windows Settings** | **Security Settings**:

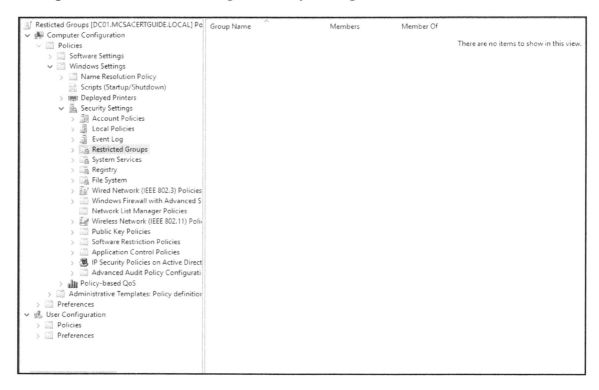

Once you navigate to **Restricted Groups**, you need to create a new Restricted Group configuration in the GPO. In the following example, MCSA 2016 group will be a member of the Administrators on all computers where this policy is applied:

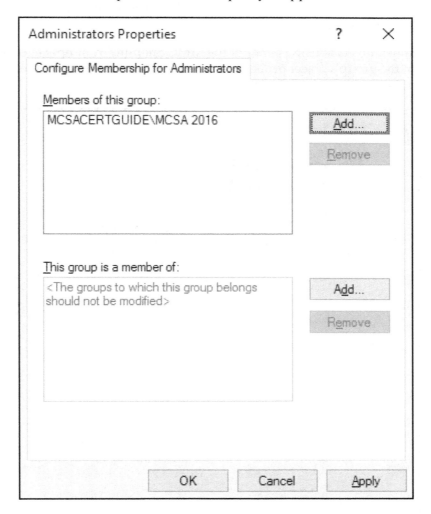

Once configured, the GPO need to be linked to the OUs that hold the computer account that needs to have this configuration.

Enumerating group memberships

In a large-scale environment, enumerating group membership is often a regular task. The reasons why we need to enumerate group membership include security compliance and analyzing access to resources.

You can accomplish this task using either of the MMC Snap-ins by simply checking the **Members** tab in the group's object properties. If you decide to use Active Directory Users and Computers, you will see the following screen:

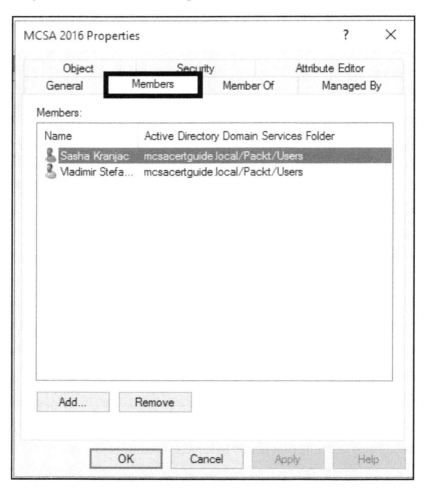

Active Directory Administrative Center is a little bit different:

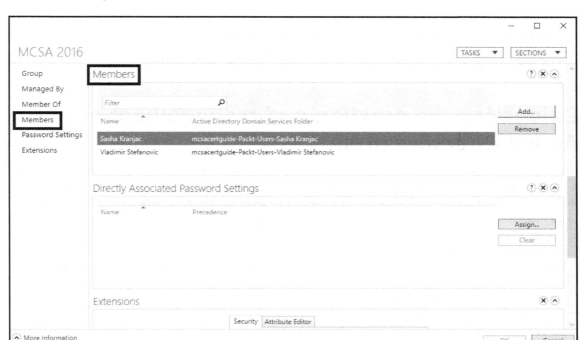

This can also be done using the Get-ADGroupMember PowerShell cmdlet:

```
Get-ADGroupMember -Identity "MCSA 2016" | Format-Table Name
```

Automating group-membership management using Windows PowerShell

In the previous sections, we mentioned that PowerShell is the best native tool in Windows operating systems for automation. Although you can select more than one user in MMC Snap-ins and add them to the same group at one time, this approach has some limitations. Using PowerShell, you can make a query against AD DS with some filtering options, such as the company name or department name, and then add those accounts to the same groups.

The following command will show you how to add a member to a group based on their company name:

```
$Members = Get-ADUser -Filter {Company -eq "Packt"}

Add-ADGroupMember -Identity "MCSA 2016" -Members $Members
```

Delegating the creation and management of Active Directory groups

Users, groups, and computers are objects in AD DS that are stored in the OU. By default, all users and groups are stored in the **Users** container and the computers are stored in the Computers container. As mentioned earlier in the chapter, OUs need to be created to consolidate objects for simplified management using GPOs linking, or delegating administrative rights. One of the rights that you can delegate to a specific user or group is **Create, delete and manage groups.** With this delegate control, specific users or group members will be able to create, delete, and manage groups in the selected OU and all other OUs in the subtree:

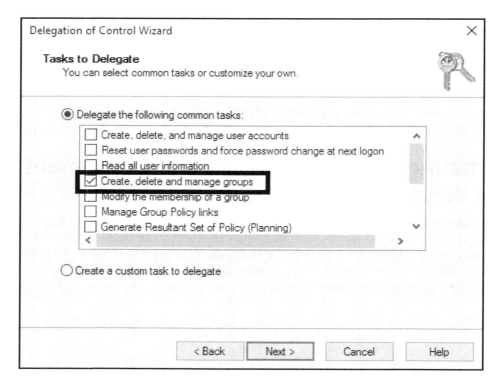

Active Directory containers

Once you've configured the domain environment and installed the first domain controller in the root domain, many AD DS objects are created. Because of the AD DS design, these need to be stored in a container or in the OU. There are several container objects that are installed by default. They don't have the same properties as other generic Active Directory containers (such as sites, domains, and OUs). You can't delete the system container, nor can you create a new system container. And you can't link GPOs to those containers.

Creating, configuring, and deleting OUs

Creating OUs is straightforward, as is the case with other objects mentioned in this chapter. It can be done using the same tools: MMC Snap-ins and PowerShell. During the creation process, you need to define the name of the OU and it will be created. Unlike other objects covered in this chapter, OUs are, by default, protected from accidental deletion, regardless of what tool is used. Using Active Directory Administrative, you will see the following screen:

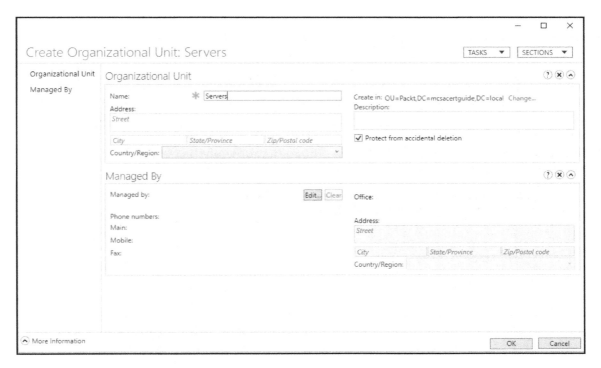

The Active Directory Users and Computers MMC Snap-in will give you a different look for the same task:

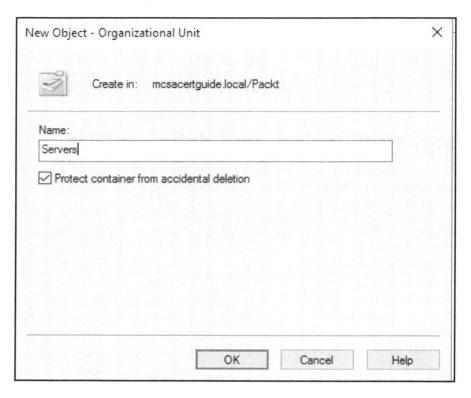

If you decide to use PowerShell, the `New-ADOrganizationalUnit` cmdlet needs to be used to create an OU:

```
New-ADOrganizationalUnit -Name Servers -Path
"OU=Packt,DC=mcsacertguide,DC=local"
```

Summary

In this chapter, we learned the most important concepts related to AD DS. We learned about logical and physical components and their functions, which tools can be used to manage AD DS, and what's new in Windows Server 2016 AD DS. We also learned how to create a new forest, how to add a new domain in an existing forest, and what RODC is and how to install it. Along with this, we covered user, group, and computer management, so you should now be able to create and manage AD DS objects.

In the next chapter, we'll cover advanced AD DS management, including AD DS Forests, AD DS Sites and Replication, and AD DS Security.

Questions

1. Which FSMO roles are forest-wide?
    1. Domain-naming master and Schema master
    2. Schema master and Infrastructure master
    3. Domain-naming master and PDC emulator
    4. Infrastructure master and PDC emulator

2. Which tool needs to be used for IFM?
    1. Active Directory Users and Computers
    2. `Ntdsutil.exe`
    3. Active Directory Administrative Center
    4. AD DS module for PowerShell

3. What is the first step in removing old domain controllers?
    1. Restart server
    2. Uninstall AD DS role
    3. Demote domain controller
    4. Move all FSMO roles to new domain controller

4. Which tools can be used to copy user accounts?
    1. Active Directory Users and Computers
    2. `Ntdsutil.exe`
    3. Active Directory Administrative Center
    4. AD DS module for PowerShell

5. Can a Global group be converted to a Domain Local group?
    1. Yes
    2. No

6. Can a Domain Local group be converted to a Universal group?
    1. Yes
    2. No

7. Which FSMO role shouldn't be deployed on the GC server?
    1. Schema master
    2. Infrastructure master
    3. Domain-naming master
    4. RID master

8. Are user accounts protected against accidental deletion by default?
    1. Yes
    2. No

9. Are OU objects protected against accidental deletion by default?
    1. Yes
    2. No

Further reading

Check out the following links for more information about AD DS:

- https://docs.microsoft.com/en-us/windows-server/identity/ad-ds/active-directory-domain-services
- https://social.technet.microsoft.com/wiki/contents/articles/699.active-directory-domain-services-ad-ds-overview.aspx
- https://docs.microsoft.com/en-us/windows/desktop/ADSchema/active-directory-schema

2
Managing and Maintaining Active Directory

In the previous chapter, we learned how to install **Active Directory Domain Services (AD DS)**, how to promote the server to the domain controller, how to install additional domain controllers or create new domains in the same forest, and how to create and manage AD DS objects, such as users, groups, and computers. Creating an Active Directory and objects, however, is just the beginning of the AD journey. Created objects must be maintained, especially in more complex environments.

In this chapter, we will cover advanced management tasks in AD DS, such as managing managed service accounts and AD DS in complex environments. We will also look into AD DS forests, AD DS security, and backing up and restoring AD DS. Each section in this chapter will give you a deep understanding of these functionalities.

In this chapter, we will cover the following topics:

- Active directory authentication and account policies
- Maintaining the active directory
- Active directory in enterprise scenarios

Active directory authentication and account policies

In this section, you will learn how to create and manage service accounts and service principal names, how to configure Kerberos constrained delegation, how to work with passwords, lockout policies, and password setting objects, how to delegate password management, and how to configure Kerberos and authentication policies.

Active Directory provides an authentication mechanism for all objects in an Active Directory, such as users and computers. Using the Kerberos authentication protocol, Active Directory can safely authenticate any user or computer against any domain in the forest.

Creating and configuring managed service accounts

In Windows operating systems, many applications need some type of administrative access to local networks and resources. In the past, administrators needed to create dedicated user accounts for specific applications to provide the application with appropriate access to the local network and resources. In most scenarios, the password for those accounts was configured so that it would never expire. Administrators had to remember or write down these passwords. This type of account required administration and could lead to potential security breaches.

 In general, this type of account doesn't need any specific administration, but if the password is set to never expire, then in most cases the password will not be changed and the account will be more vulnerable.

In Windows Server 2016, AD DS objects, known as **managed service accounts (MSAs)**, became fully supported. MSAs were first introduced in Windows Server 2008 R2. The idea behind creating MSAs was to reduce possible security issues and to eliminate the need to manually administer accounts and their credentials. Using MSAs also means that we no longer have to use the system service accounts, that is, the local service, local system, and network service. MSAs are stored in AD DS as `msDS-ManagedServiceAccount` objects. Structurally, this class is inherited from the `User` class, which gives MSAs all user-like functions, such as authentication. MSAs use the same password update mechanism as computer objects in AD DS, and the whole process does not require user intervention. MSAs require Windows Server 2008 R2 or later, .NET Framework 3.5.x, and the AD DS PowerShell module.

In Windows Server 2016, you can configure **group MSAs (gMSAs)**. Standard MSAs cannot provide MSA functionality to services that are running on more than one server, such as a web server farm, while gMSAs give you the ability to configure multiple servers to use the same MSAs. All of the benefits of MSAs, such as automatic password maintenance and simplified SPN management, are still included in gMSAs. gMSA objects contain a list of computers or groups that can retrieve the MSA password from AD DS. Once they retrieve the password from AD DS, they can authenticate services with MSA.

1. The first step in configuring MSAs is to configure the **Key Distribution Service (KDS)** root key. This needs to be done using the following PowerShell commands:

   ```
   Add-KdsRootKey -EffectiveImmediately
   Add-KdsRootKey -EffectiveTime (Get-Date).AddHours((-10))
   ```

   Without the `-EffectiveImmediately` switch, you would need to wait for up to 10 hours, which is the default time for replication to other domain controllers when you create a new `KDSRootKey`. With the `-EffectiveImmediately` switch, the actual effective time is set to 10 hours later than the current time. For testing purposes, you can bypass this functionality by setting the `-EffectiveTime` parameter to 10 hours before the current time.

2. Once you create the KDS root key, you can create a new MSA using the `New-ADServiceAccount` PowerShell cmdlet with the `PrinicipalsAllowedToRetrieveManagedPassword` parameter. This parameter accepts one or more comma-separated computer accounts or groups that can retrieve passwords from AD DS for MSA.

3. If you want to create a new managed service account using PowerShell, use the following command:

   ```
   New-ADServiceAccount -DNSHostName DC01 -Name WebFarmMSA
   -PrincipalsAllowedToRetrieveManagedPassword SRV01$, SRV02$
   ```

Once you run following PowerShell command, you will be able to see created MSA in Managed Services Account OU, like shown in the following screenshot:

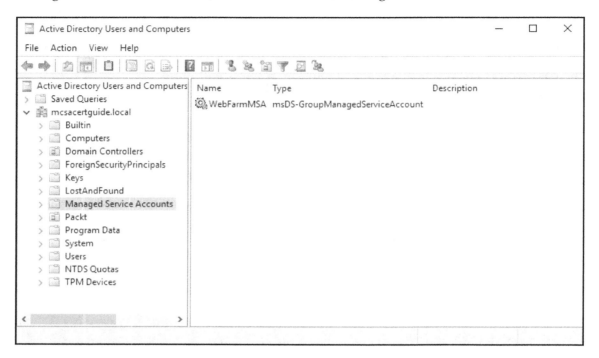

 The dollar sign ($) needs to be added if a computer account is defined as an AD DS object that can retrieve the MSA password from AD DS.

Once you have created and configured MSA, you need to install MSA on computers that are defined in the `-PrinicipalsAllowedToRetrieveManagedPassword` parameter during the creation process before you start to use it. This needs to be done using the following PowerShell command:

```
Install-ADServiceAccount -Identity WebFarmMSA
```

 All servers that need to install MSA need to have .NET Framework 3.5.x and the AD DS PowerShell module installed.

When you have installed MSA on the computer, you can configure the services to use it. You need to edit the properties of the service and change the login parameters in the **Log On** tab, as shown in the following screenshot:

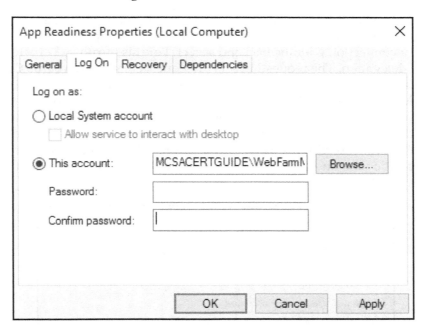

The MSA account needs to be added to the **Log On** tab in the service properties in the following format: MCSACERTGUIDE\WebFarmMSA$. The password field should be left blank.

Configuring Kerberos Constrained Delegation (KCD)

Regardless of the size of the environment, some scenarios might require a service to make a connection with another service on behalf of the client. For example, the frontend server needs to make a connection with the backend server. For this purpose, Kerberos uses authentication delegation. The requesting service requests that the **Kerberos Constrained Delegation** (**KDC**) authorize the second service to act on its behalf. Later, the second service can delegate authentication to a third service. For security purposes, from Windows Server 2008 onward, Microsoft added a new feature called **constrained delegation**. This feature limits the scope of services that can be delegated and provides a safer delegation function. With this functionality, you can configure the delegation to a specific service account or a specific set of instances running on a specific computer, as shown in the following screenshot:

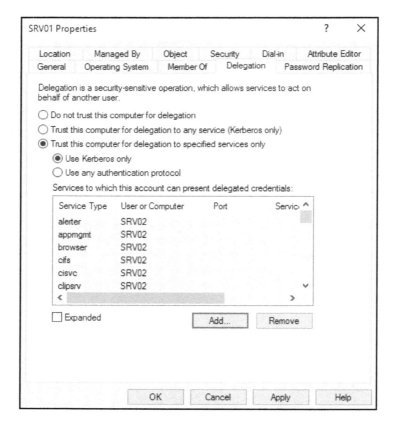

Managing service principal names (SPNs)

A SPN is a unique identifier for each instance of a service running on a computer that is registered in AD DS and associated with a service account specified by SPN. A service's SPN is used when the service needs to authenticate another service, and that SPN distinguishes it from other services on the computer. Before the Kerberos authentication service can use an SPN to authenticate a service, the SPN must be registered on the account object that the service instance uses to log on.

There are several ways to check which SPNs are assigned to an object. You can check this by using **MMC Snap-ins** and checking the `servicePrincipalName` attribute, or you can use the `setspn` command-line tool :

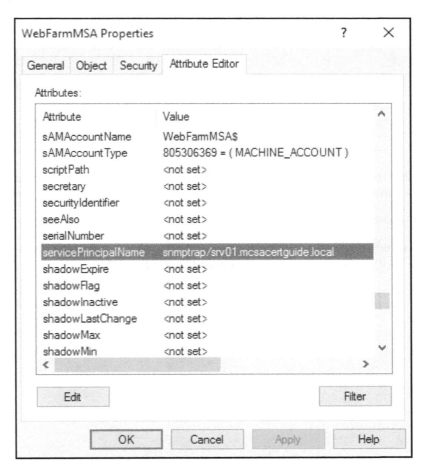

Once you double-click on the `servicePrincipalName` attribute, you will be able to check and edit the values for the attribute:

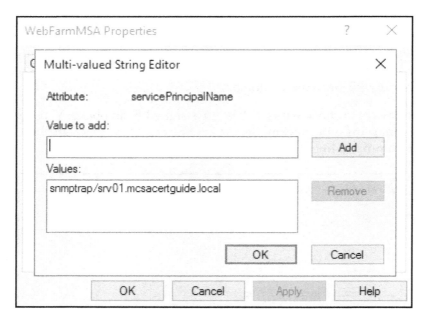

If you want to list the SPNs that are registered to MSA, you need to run the following command in Command Prompt:

```
setspn -l WebRarmMSA$
```

If the SPN is not registered to a service account, you can register it using the `setspn` command-line tool, with the command in the following format:

```
setspn -s <service name>/<server FQDN> <domain name>\<service account name>
setspn -s snmptrap/srv01.mcsacertguide.local mcsacertguide\WebFarmMSA$
```

Using the `-s` switch, you can make sure that a duplicate SPN does not exist.

Configuring domain and local user password policy settings

One of the most important security tasks in the domain environment is password policy configuration. The password policy defines how strong a user's password will be. A stronger password policy makes your domain environment more resilient against security breaches. Although Windows Server has configured a default password policy in the default domain GPO, you can reconfigure the settings and align parameters according to your company's policies.

The parameters that are included and configured in the password policy are as follows:

- **Enforce password history**: The number of unique passwords that must be associated with a user's account before an old password can be reused. The default value is **24**.
- **Maximum password age**: The number of days that a user can use a password for before they must change it. The default value is **42**.
- **Minimum password age**: The number of days that a password must be used before the user can change it. The default value is **1**.
- **Minimum password length**: The minimum number of characters that a user's password must contain. The default value is **7**.
- **Complexity requirements**: This defines how complex a user's password must be. A complex password must contain three or four of the following types of characters:
    - Uppercase letters [A–Z]
    - Lowercase letters [a–z]
    - Numerals [0–9]
    - Special, non-alphanumeric characters, such as !@#)(*&^%
- **Store passwords using reversible encryption**: This determines whether the operating system stores passwords using reversible encryption. It provides support for applications that use protocols that require knowledge of the user's password for authentication purposes. For security reasons, this configuration is disabled by default, and shouldn't be enabled if it is not necessary.

These settings are stored in the default domain policy, as mentioned earlier, and can be changed. You just need to edit the GPO parameters under **Computer Configuration** I **Windows Settings** I **Security Settings** I **Account Policies** I **Password Policy**:

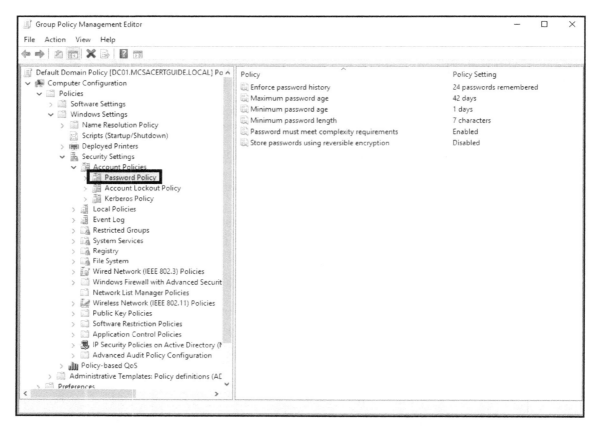

Configuring and applying Password Settings Objects (PSOs)

Windows Server 2008 came with one important security feature related to the password policy. The administrator can now define more than one password policy in a domain. Before Windows Server 2008, if you wanted to implement two different password policies, you had to configure an additional domain, because one password policy per domain was allowed. Fine-grained password policies give you control over user password requirements and you can create many different password policies and assign them to specific users or groups. This is useful, for example, if you want to configure a stronger password policy for administrator accounts than the domain users, or if you want to configure a non-complex password policy for guest accounts.

To support this fine-grained password policy feature, AD DS includes two object types:

- **Password Settings Container**: This is a container that is created by default. It stores PSOs that you create.
- **PSOs**: This defines specific password policies that are linked to a specific user or group. Only members of the Domain Admins group can create and configure PSOs.

The creation and configuration of PSOs can be done using the Active Directory Administrative Center MMC's Snap-in or the `New-ADFineGrainedPasswordPolicy` PowerShell cmdlet . If you want to use the Active Directory Administrative Center to configure this feature, you need to open the system container, where you will find **Password Settings Container**. You can then create and configure a new PSO:

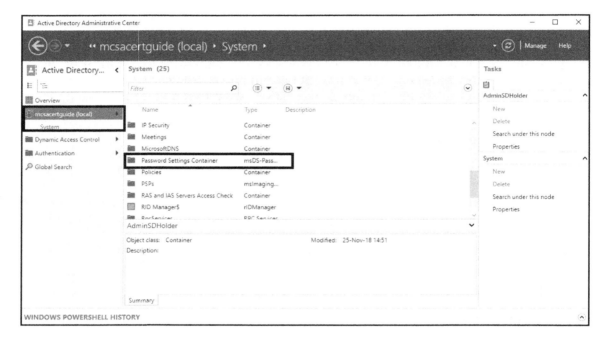

Once you navigate to **Password Setting Container**, you can create a new PSO, as shown in the following screenshot:

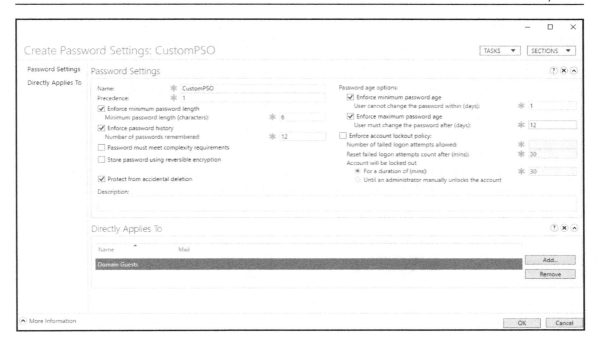

If you decided to implement this feature using PowerShell, you need to run the following commands:

```
New-ADFineGrainedPasswordPolicy CustomPSO -ComplexityEnabled:$false -
MaxPasswordAge:"12.00:00:00" -MinPasswordAge:"1.00:00:00" -
MinPasswordLength:"6" -PasswordHistoryCount:"12" -Precedence:"1" -
ReversibleEncryptionEnabled:$false -ProtectedFromAccidentalDeletion:$true

Add-ADFineGrainedPasswordPolicySubject CustomPSO -Subjects "Domain Guests"
```

Delegating password settings management

By default, only members of the Domain Admins group can manage settings in the password policy and the fine-grained password policy. If you want, you can delegate this ability to other users.

To delegate permissions to other users so that you can change the settings in the domain password policy, you need to delegate permissions to the user to change the default domain GPO, because the domain password policy is configured in that GPO by default. You can do that by adding a specific user or group in the delegation tab under the GPO settings and giving them the appropriate permissions. You need to perform the following steps:

1. Open the **Group Policy Management** console.
2. Select the desired GPO.
3. On the **Delegation** tab, add the appropriate user or group and define the permissions, as shown in the following screenshot:

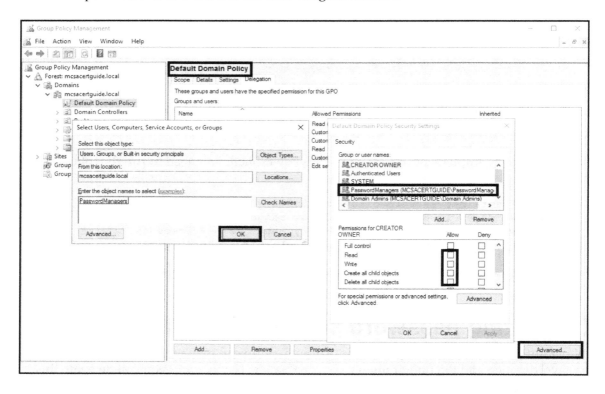

4. Once you add an appropriate user or group for permission delegation, you need to define the permissions:

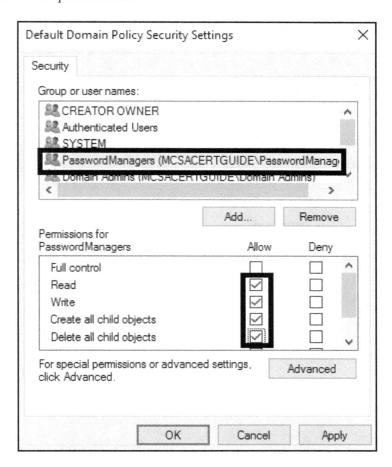

5. To delegate permissions to create and manage PSOs, you need to give permissions to the user or the group in the Active Directory Administrative Center MMC Snap-in by adding the appropriate permissions to **Password Settings Container** under the **System** container:

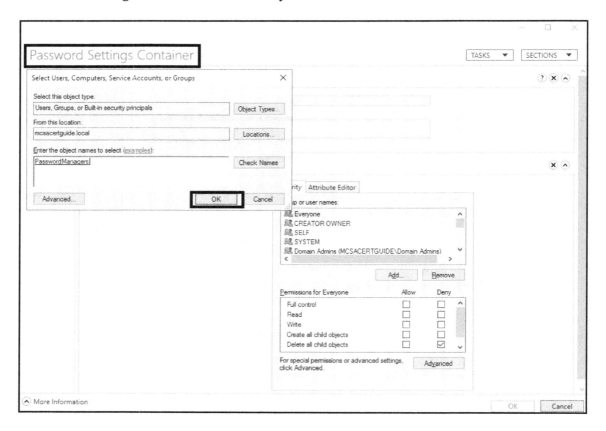

Configuring account lockout policy settings

This setting is not configured by default and the recommendation is to enable this policy. Password policies specify how strong a user's password has to be, while the account lockout policies define whether the accounts should be locked if there are too many invalid sign-in attempts. This setting needs to be configured in the same GPO as a password policy and you need to define some thresholds:

- **Account lockout duration**: The number of minutes that a locked account remains locked

- **Account lockout threshold**: The number of failed sign-in attempts that are allowed before a user account is locked out
- **Reset account lockout counter after**: How much time must elapse after a failed sign-in attempt before sign-in is allowed

If you want to configure these settings, you just need to edit the GPO parameters under **Computer Configuration** | **Windows Settings** | **Security Settings** | **Account Policies** | **Account Lockout Policy**, as follows:

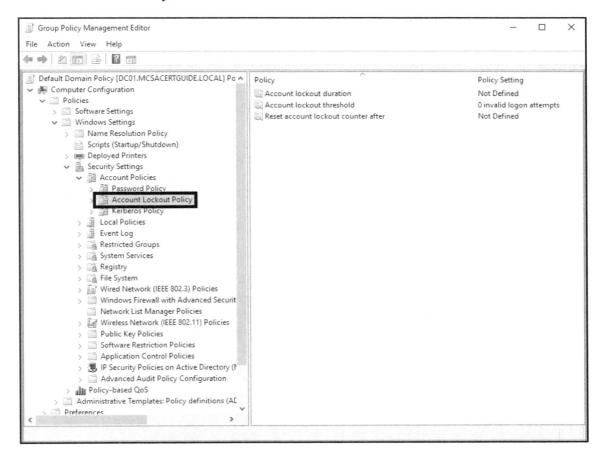

Enabling and configuring this policy will secure your domain environment from brute-force or dictionary attacks.

Configuring the Kerberos policy settings within the group policy

As we mentioned in the previous chapter, Kerberos is the default authentication protocol in Windows domain environments for all objects that need to be authenticated. In the GPO, you can find the Kerberos-related policy that defines Kerberos-related settings, such as ticket lifetimes and enforcement. The Kerberos policy contains settings for **ticket-granting ticket (TGT)**, the session ticket lifetimes, and timestamp settings. In most scenarios, the default values are appropriate.

However, if you want to make some changes in Kerberos policy, you can change following settings:

- **Enforcing user logon restrictions**: This determines whether the KDC will validate every session ticket request against the user account's user rights policy. By default, this is enabled.
- **Maximum lifetime for service ticket**: The maximum time a service ticket is valid for authenticating client access to a service. If a service ticket expires before the client initiates the connection, the server will respond with an error and the client will be redirected to KDC to receive a new service ticket. The default value is **600** minutes.
- **Maximum lifetime for user ticket**: The amount of time that the user account's TGT is valid. The default value is **10** hours.
- **Maximum lifetime for user ticket renewal**: The amount of time for which the user account's TGT can be renewed. The default value is **7** days.
- **Maximum tolerance for computer clock synchronization**: The amount of time that the client computer clock can be out of sync with the domain controller. If the difference is larger than the configured value, authentication will not be possible. The default value is **5** minutes.

If you want to change these settings, you just need to edit the GPO parameters under **Computer Configuration** | **Windows Settings** | **Security Settings** | **Account Policies** | **Kerberos Policy**, as shown in the following screenshot:

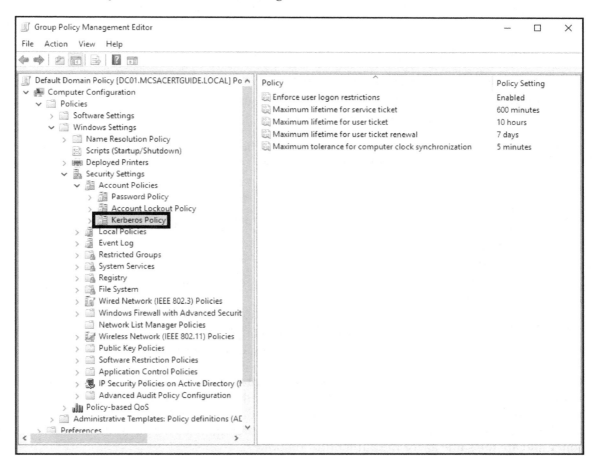

Configuring authentication policies

The principles of authentication policies came with Windows Server 2012 R2. These allow you to configure more restrictive Kerberos settings for a specific user, computer, or service accounts.

Implementing authentication policies requires the following:

- All domain controllers must be Windows Server 2012 R2 or newer
- The domain functional level must be Windows Server 2012 R2 or newer
- Domain controllers must support DAC

When you are configuring authentication policies in the Active Directory Administrative Center, you need to configure the following settings:

- Display name.
- Description.
- Purpose of the policy; by default, the policy is enforced but can be configured for audit purposes.
- Accounts to which the policy applies.
- For user, service, and computer accounts, you can define the following settings separately:
  - The TGT lifetime of the account
  - Access control conditions using DAC claims that define which users or services can run on which devices

Authentication policy silos are containers that can contain user, computer, and services accounts. These accounts can be managed by using authentication policies which can then be assigned to authentication policy silos. The authentication policy silo can be created based on the requirements of your organization. The prerequisites for the authentication policy silo are the same as for the authentication policy.

For more information regarding authentication policies and silos, check out the following link: https://docs.microsoft.com/en-us/windows-server/security/credentials-protection-and-management/authentication-policies-and-authentication-policy-silos.

Maintaining AD

In this section, you will learn how to back up and restore the AD, how to manage the AD offline, how to configure the password replication policy for the **Read Only Domain Controller** (**RODC**), and how to monitor and manage AD replication.

Backing up AD and SYSVOL

Like other servers, the AD and the domain controllers need to be backed up. A user account could be deleted either intentionally or accidentally. This will result in the user's inability to log in to the system and use resources. Although a new user account can be created with the same name and parameters, from an Active Directory perspective, this account would be a completely new account and the rights that the deleted account had cannot be transferred to a new account. By backing up AD, you will be able to restore the user account and bring it back to a fully operational status.

In the past, backing up involved creating system state backups. Nowadays, with Windows Server 2016, the system state backup is much larger than it was previously and can vary with regard to many different factors, so it is part of the full server backup. Windows Servers have a native backup tool called Windows Server Backup. This feature is included with all Windows Servers and can be used and configured with the MMC Snap-in, the `wbadmin` command-line tools, or PowerShell. You can use Windows Server Backup to back up the following:

- The full server (all volumes)
- Selected volumes
- Selected items, such as specific folders or the system state

Installing Windows Server Backup is a straightforward process. Once you have installed the backup feature, you need to schedule a full backup of your domain controllers.

Restoring AD

The backup process for AD DS and the domain controller is not that complicated, but if you need to restore AD DS from a previously taken backup, you need to be aware of the different types of restore procedures that exist.

The domain controller or AD DS can experience corruption, damage, or failure. To restore AD DS, you must restart the domain controller in DSRM to get full access to the files. Once you are logged in to DSRM, you can start the restoration process. There are two different types of AD DS restoration: **authoritative** and **non-authoritative**.

Non-authoritative restoration

This type or restoration is useful when one of the domain controllers of the AD DS database is damaged or corrupted. In this scenario, you need to restore the domain controller from a known good state backup. After the restoration process, the domain controller will contact other domain controllers and request all of the necessary updates from them.

In a scenario in which you need to perform a non-authoritative restoration, it is very important that restored files are not older than 180 days, which is the default tombstone lifetime. In the Active Directory environment, replication between domain controllers will fail if you try to replicate data to a domain controller where the AD objects are older than the tombstone lifetime value.

Authoritative restoration

Authoritative restoration is necessary when the restored object from the backup must be replicated to the other domain controllers in the domain. The most common scenario in which authoritative restoration is required is restoring a deleted object, such as a user or a group. The restoration process requires you to mark objects that you want to retain as authoritative. After the restart, the object will replicate from the restored domain controller to all replication partners.

With Windows Server 2008 R2, you can restore deleted objects from the AD Recycle Bin, if this feature is enabled. If AD Recycle Bin is not enabled, or you have a later operating system, you will need to perform a manual restoration process with the `ntdsutil` command-line tool. In this section, we will describe the restoration process using `ntdsutil` and the Active Directory Recycle Bin.

Managing the AD offline

In older versions of Windows Server, some maintenance tasks with the AD DS database required you to restart the domain controller in **Directory Services Restore Mode (DSRM)**. Windows Server 2012, however, came with the concept of restartable AD DS. This allows you to stop and start the AD DS without restarting the domain controller, meaning that you can now perform maintenance tasks much more quickly. This functionality doesn't require any specific functional level or prerequisites. You just need to open the **Services** console or use PowerShell to stop and start the AD DS service.

For a system state restoration of AD DS, you still need to restart the domain controller in DSRM and perform either an authoritative or non-authoritative restoration.

Performing the offline defragmentation of an AD database

One of the most common AD DS database maintenance tasks is offline defragmentation.

Although Active Directory performs online defragmentation every 12 hours as an automated process, this does not reclaim space in the AD database after cleaning up old objects. By performing offline defragmentation, the ntds.dit file will be reduced and all database indexes will be re-indexed.

Restartable AD DS allows you to perform this task in just a couple of minutes. You need to stop the AD DS service and run the following command using the ntdsutil command-line tool:

```
NtdsUtil.exe
activate instance NTDS
files
compact to C:\
```

The following screenshot shows the output of the preceding command:

```
Administrator: Command Prompt - ntdsutil.exe                      —    □    ×

Microsoft Windows [Version 10.0.14393]
(c) 2016 Microsoft Corporation. All rights reserved.

C:\Windows\system32>ntdsutil.exe
ntdsutil.exe: activate instance ntds
Active instance set to "ntds".
ntdsutil.exe: files
file maintenance: compact to c:\
Initiating DEFRAGMENTATION mode...
    Source Database: C:\Windows\NTDS\ntds.dit
    Target Database: c:\ntds.dit

            Defragmentation  Status (% complete)

        0    10   20   30   40   50   60   70   80   90  100
        |----|----|----|----|----|----|----|----|----|----|
        ..................................................

It is recommended that you immediately perform a full backup
of this database. If you restore a backup made before the
defragmentation, the database will be rolled back to the state
it was in at the time of that backup.

Compaction is successful. You need to:
    copy "c:\ntds.dit" "C:\Windows\NTDS\ntds.dit"
and delete the old log files:
    del C:\Windows\NTDS\*.log

file maintenance: _
```

Once this is complete, you just need to copy the defragmented database to the original location and delete the old log files with the following commands:

```
copy "c:\ntds.dit" "C:\Windows\NTDS\ntds.dit"
del C:\Windows\NTDS\*.log
```

Then, you can start the AD DS service.

Configuring AD snapshots

Creating AD snapshots can be helpful if you need to browse the content of the AD DS database from a specific period of time. Snapshots, however, should not be thought of as replacements for AD DS backup.

Use the following commands to create a snapshot of AD DS:

```
NtdsUtil.exe
activate instance ntds
snapshot
Create
```

The snapshot process can be scheduled by creating a Task Scheduler job using the appropriate ntdsutil commands.

Once the snapshot has been created, it can be browsed, but before that, it needs to be mounted. To mount the created snapshot, you need to use the ntdsutil command-line tool and list all the available snapshots. When you decide on which snapshot needs to be mounted, you can use the snapshot GUID to mount it:

```
NtdsUtil.exe
activate instance ntds
snapshot
list all
mount <GUID>
```

When the snapshot is mounted, you need to use the dsadmin command-line tool to activate the additional AD DS instances on different ports to connect to and browse the AD DS database:

```
dsamain -dbpath c:\$snap_datetime_volumec$\windows\ntds\ntds.dit -ldapport
50000
```

The following screenshot shows the output of the preceding command:

```
Administrator: Command Prompt - dsamain  -dbpath C:\$SNAP_201812091444_VOLUMEC$\windows\ntds\ntds.dit -ldapport 50000
Microsoft Windows [Version 10.0.14393]
(c) 2016 Microsoft Corporation. All rights reserved.

C:\Windows\system32>ntdsutil
ntdsutil: activate instance ntds
Active instance set to "ntds".
ntdsutil: snapshot
snapshot: create
Creating snapshot...
Snapshot set {465046df-a7a8-4903-85c9-49cb7ee843a7} generated successfully.
snapshot: list all
 1:  2018/12/09:14:44 {465046df-a7a8-4903-85c9-49cb7ee843a7}
 2:      C: {fd0a7fe7-0100-4e06-8203-c495bbb31910}

snapshot: mount 465046df-a7a8-4903-85c9-49cb7ee843a7
Snapshot {fd0a7fe7-0100-4e06-8203-c495bbb31910} mounted as C:\$SNAP_201812091444_VOLUMEC$\
snapshot: quit
ntdsutil: quit

C:\Windows\system32>dsamain -dbpath C:\$SNAP_201812091444_VOLUMEC$\windows\ntds\ntds.dit -ldapport 50000
EVENTLOG (Informational): NTDS General / Service Control : 1000
Microsoft Active Directory Domain Services startup complete
```

 `C:\$snap_datetime_volumec$\` will vary depending on the snapshot. This is a mount point on your local drive and it will be shown after the mounting process. You can also check your local drive at any time to see the mounted location.

If you want to view the mounted and activated snapshots, you need to perform the following steps:

1. Open the Active Directory Users and Computers MMC Snap-in
2. Connect to the mounted AD DS database by entering the server name and port combination that is used in the dsadmin command

In the following screenshot, you can see an example of how to connect to an AD DS snapshot:

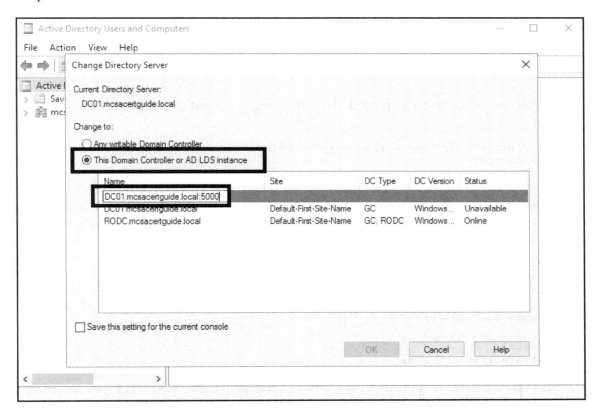

Performing object-level and container-level recovery

If you need to restore objects from an AD DS backup, you can do this on either the object-level or the container-level. Of course, in most scenarios, this needs to be done as an authoritative restoration due to the accidental deletion of one or more objects. First of all, you need to restart the server in DSRM and restore a backup from any previous known state, based on your requirements. This can be done using the Windows Server Backup MMC Snap-in or the `wbadmin` command-line tool.

To list the available backups, you need to run the following command:

```
wbadmin get versions -backuptarget:D: -machine:DC01
```

 The machine name and the drive letter will vary depending on the configuration.

When you decide which backup needs to be restored, you need to run the following command:

```
wbadmin start systemstaterecovery -version:<version> -backuptarget:D: -
machine:DC01
```

Once you have restored the backup, before restarting, you need to mark the object for authoritative restoration. Otherwise, the object will not be restored as authoritative and all subsequent changes will be pulled from its replication partners. For this task, you need to use the ntdsutil command-line tool:

```
ntdsutil
activate instance ntds
authoritative restore
restore object "CN=Vladimir,OU=Packt,DC=mcsacertguide,DC=local" (if you
restore one object)

ntdsutil
activate instance ntds
authoritative restore
restore subtree "OU=IT,OU=Packt,DC=mcsacertguide,DC=local" (if you restore
complete organizational unit and all objects)
```

AD Recycle Bin (configuring and restoring objects)

From Windows Server 2008, a new AD DS feature called AD Recycle Bin is available. With this feature, the restoration process of deleted objects is much simpler. Administrators can restore deleted objects to their full functionality without having to restore the AD data from backups or manually mark objects for authoritative restore, which was the process we explained previously. The AD Recycle Bin is not enabled by default; you need to enable it using the Active Directory Administrative Center MMC Snap-in or the `Enable-ADOptionalFeature` PowerShell command. Once enabled, the AD Recycle Bin feature cannot be removed later:

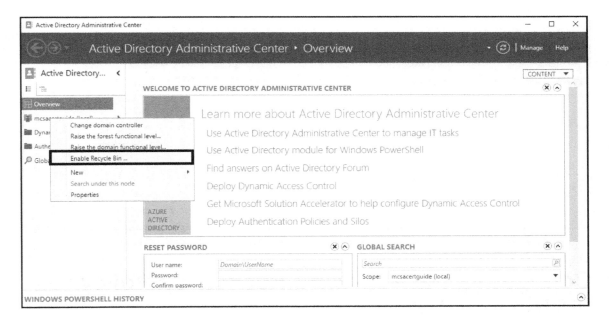

After you enable the AD Recycle Bin, when an AD object is deleted, the system preserves all of the object's link-valued and non–link-valued attributes and the object becomes logically deleted and moved to the **Deleted Objects** container. A deleted object will remain in the container during the duration of the deleted object lifetime. The msDS-deletedObjectLifetime attribute determines the deleted object lifetime, which, by default, is 180 days. Once recovered from the AD Recycle Bin, the object will be part of the same groups that it was prior to deletion:

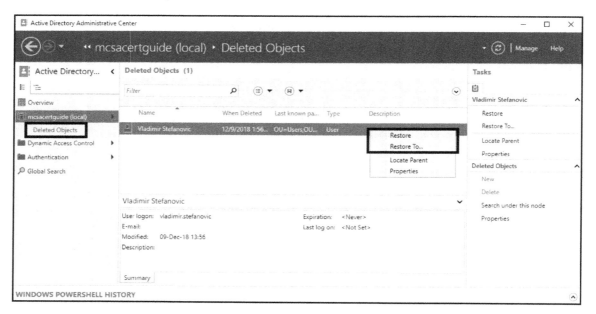

Configuring the Password Replication Policy (PRP) for RODC

In the RODC context, the password replication policy determines which users' or computers' credentials will be cached on the RODC. If the password replication policy allows the RODC to cache a user's credentials, that user will be authenticated on the RODC. Otherwise, all authentication requests will be forwarded to writable domain controllers. By default, there are two security groups that define password replication to RODC:

- **Allowed RODC password replication group**: This group doesn't contain any objects by default

- **Denied RODC password replication group**: By default, the members of this group include Domain Admins, Enterprise Admins, and Group Policy Creator Owners

If you want to configure the PRP based on your requirements, you can do that by editing the configuration on the RODC computer account in AD DS, as shown in the following screenshot:

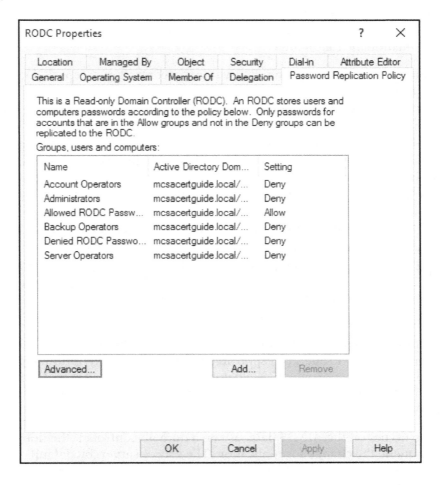

You can add a specific user, group, or computer account to a policy or remove them. You can also check which passwords for accounts are already cached on the RODC.

Monitoring and managing replication

Replication between domain controllers is one of the most important processes in the AD DS environment. AD DS replication will ensure that each partition on the domain controller is consistent with the partitions on all other domain controllers. The characteristics of AD DS replication include the following:

- **Multiple master replication**: Every domain controller, except RODC, can make changes.
- **Pull replication**: The domain controller requests, or pulls, change from other domain controllers.
- **Store-and-forward replication**: The domain controller replicates changes that are pulled from the domain controller to other domain controllers in the environment.
- **Automatic generation**: Automatic generation of an efficient and robust replication topology.
- **Attribute-level replication**: Only attributes that have been changed and their descriptive metadata will be replicated.
- **Collision detection and management**: Although it is possible, changing a single object at the same time on different domain controllers is rare. However, most of the time, AD DS algorithms can solve this issue, or, in the worst-case scenario, you would need to reconcile these changes.

The AD DS component known as **Knowledge Consistency Checker (KCC)**, which is hosted on each domain controller, is responsible for generating and optimizing replication between domain controllers on site. KCC evaluates domain controllers and creates two-way connections with three-hop robust topology. KCC runs every 15 minutes by default, but you can specify intervals based on your requirements.

When a change occurs on the AD DS database on a domain controller, the domain controller will queue the change for replication. The source server, by default, waits 15 seconds before notifying replication partners. Once the replication partner receives and processes the change, it will wait for three seconds before notifying the downstream partners. These delays, the initial delay and all subsequent delays, in a large environment can cause higher network traffic.

The most commonly used tools for monitor replication are `repadmin` and `dcdiag`. **Repadmin** is a command-line tool that allows you to report the status of replication on each domain controller, while **Dcdiag** performs numerous tests and reports on the overall health of replication and security for AD DS. The most common commands include the following:

- `repadmin /showrepl`
- `repadmin /showconn`
- `repadmin /kcc`
- `dcdiag /test:dns`

 For more information about the `repadmin` tool, visit the following link at `https://social.technet.microsoft.com/wiki/contents/articles/ 50788.active-directory-repadmin-tool.aspx`.

AD in enterprise scenarios

In this section, we will learn how to configure multi-domain and forest infrastructures, upgrade existing infrastructures, configure forest trust, and implement and manage AD sites.

Configuring a multi-domain and multi-forest AD infrastructure

Although many organizations adequately operate inside single domains and forests, some organizations are yet to implement multi-domain or even multi-forest organization. As we mentioned in `Chapter 1`, *Installing and Configuring Active Directory*, AD DS domains and forests provide different types of boundaries, and those boundaries might be a reason why you should start thinking about multi-domain or multi-forest deployment. If you want to separate the DNS namespace, administrative access, or domain replication, your organization is a good candidate for multi-domain environment. Other reasons why you might want to implement a multi-forest environment include if your schema is incompatible with a new planned application, if you want to completely isolate your security, or if need to align to multinational requirements.

However, both of these complex AD DS environments bring some challenges related to configuration and management. Regardless of whether you need to deploy a multi-domain or multi-forest AD DS environment, the domains and forests need to trust each other if you want to provide access to the network and resources to users in different domains. Unlike forest trusts, which need to be configured manually, trusts between domains in multi-domain environments are configured automatically during the configuration of the new domain. In multi-domain environments, you need to decide which type of domain relationship is better for you. You need to choose between a parent-child model in the same domain tree, or an additional domain in a new tree in the same forest. In both models, domain trust is automatically configured as two-way transitive trust. Forest trust configuration will be describe later in this section.

The process of installing a new domain controller in a new domain was covered in the previous chapter.

Upgrading existing domains and forests

In the previous chapter, we described the process of upgrading domain controllers and domains. There are two possible options: migration and in-place upgrades. Both of these concepts have pros and cons, and only you can decide which is the better option for your organization. Basically, the approach for upgrading domains and forests is the same, except for one difference. You need to perform an upgrade on all domain controllers in the domain and forest. Once you upgrade all the domain controllers to the new version and demote the old domain controllers (if you are performing migration), the last step is to raise the domain and the forest's functional level.

Configuring the domain and forest functional levels

Domain and forest levels define a set of functionalities that the domain and forest have. Some features are not available and cannot be implemented if your domain and forest levels are below the required level. For example, the AD Recycle Bin cannot be implemented if your domain and forest levels are not at Windows Server 2008 R2 or higher.

Upgrading domain and forest levels is a one-way process. Once the level has been raised, it cannot be downgraded. The process is simple and can be done using MMC Snap-ins or PowerShell. Before you start raising the domain and the forest level, however, you need to know that the highest level must match your oldest operating system on the domain controller. For example, if you have five domain controllers on Windows Server 2016 and one domain controller on Windows Server 2012 R2, your highest possible domain and forest level is Windows Server 2012 R2.

The domain level can be raised using **Active Directory Users and Computers** MMC Snap-in or the `Set-ADDomainMode` PowerShell cmdlet. If you need to do this using the Active Directory Users and Computers MMC Snap-in, you need to select the option that's shown in the following screenshot:

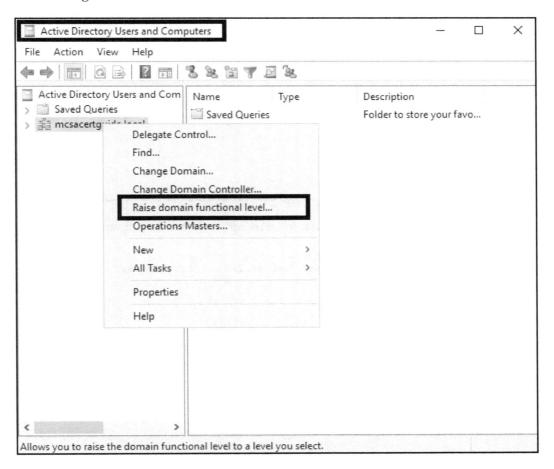

If you want to change the domain functional level using PowerShell, you need to run the following command:

```
Set-ADDomainMode -Identity mcsacertguide.local -DomainMode
Windows2016Domain
```

The forest level can be raised using the **Active Directory Domains and Trusts** MMC Snap-in or the `Set-ADForestMode` PowerShell cmdlet:

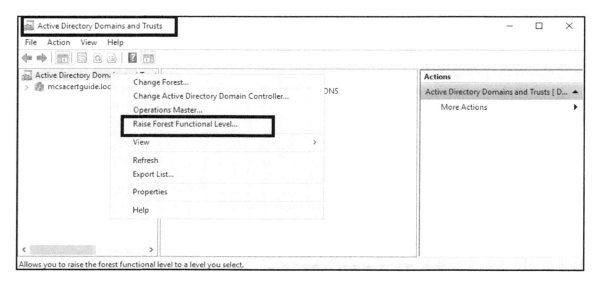

If you want to change the forest functional level using PowerShell, you need to run the following command:

```
Set-ADForestMode -Identity mcsacertguide.local -ForestMode
Windows2016Forest
```

Configuring multiple user principal name (UPN) suffixes

In multi-domain environments, the signing-in process is more complicated for users, because they need to be aware of the domain name. Although users can sign in with the NetBIOS domain name and their SAM account name, the UPN is more user-friendly because it uses the same format as the email address. Sometimes, if you have a deep forest infrastructure, the user's UPN might be more complex. For example, if your domain name is `uk.eu.mcsacertguide.local`, the user's UPN will be `vladimir@uk.eu.mcsacertguide.local`. If you want to avoid confusion and make the UPN easier to remember, you just need to create an additional UPN suffix and configure the user's account to use that suffix.

This can be done using the **Active Directory Domains and Trusts** MMC Snap-in or a PowerShell. If you want to use GUI to perform this action, you need to follow the next steps:

1. Open **Active Directory Domains and Trusts** console
2. Right click to **Active Directory Domains and Trusts** and select **Properties**
3. In box **Alternative UPN suffixes**, add desired UPN suffix, like as on image below

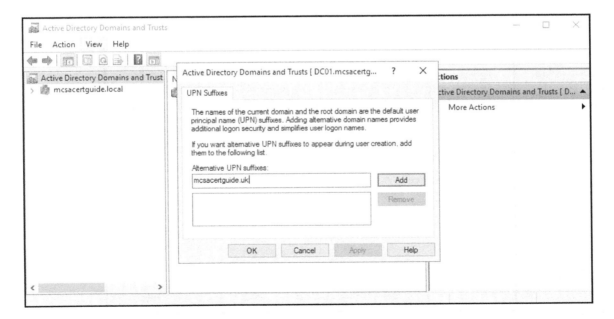

If you want to use PowerShell to configure the additional UPN suffix, you need to run the following command:

```
Set-ADForest -Identity mcsacertguide.local -UPNSuffixes
@{Add="mcsacertguide.uk"}
```

Once you have added the additional UPN suffix, you just need to change the user's UPN in their AD DS account:

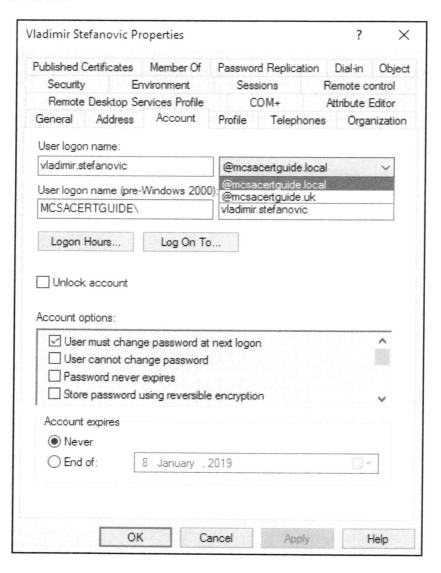

Configuring external, forest, shortcut, and realm trusts

Trusts in AD DS allow access to resources in different domains in complex AD DS environments. In a single domain, you will not face issues regarding delegating access to resources, but in complex environments, without trusts, this is impossible. There are a few different types of trusts, and each has its own set of functionalities:

Trust type	Direction	Transitivity	Description
Parent-child	Two-way	Transitive	When you add a new domain in the same forest and configure it as a parent-child domain, this trust will be automatically created.
Tree-root	Two-way	Transitive	When you create a new domain in a new tree, but in the same forest, this type of trust will be automatically created.
External	One-way, Two-way	Non-transitive	This trust enables resource access to a Windows NT 4.0 domain or an AD DS domain in another forest and needs to be configured manually.
Forest	One-way, Two-way	Transitive	This trust type needs to be used between two forests to provide access and share resources.
Realm	One-way, Two-way	Transitive or non-transitive	This trust can be configured between the Windows AD DS domain or any Kerberos v5 realm to provide access to resources.
Shortcut	One-way, Two-way	Non-transitive	This trust can be configured to improve the access between domains that are parts of different forests.

As you can see in the preceding table, the trust between domains can be one-way or two-way. This defines whether both domains can access resources in the other domain or not. Trusts can be transitive or non-transitive. If a trust is transitive, the trust between the domain will be chained. For example, if domain **A** trusts domain **B**, and domain **B** trusts domain **C**, then domain **A** trusts domain **C**.

Because trusts between domains in the same forest are automatically configured, the focus in this chapter will be on forest trust. By design, forest trusts are transitive, but you can define whether they will be one-way or two-way. Forest trust allows authenticated users from one forest to access resources from another forest if they have granted rights. Forest trusts provide the simplified management of resources across two forests, two-way trust relationships with every domain in each forest, and UPN authentication across two forests. If you have created a forest trust between **Forest A** and **Forest B**, and then you create a trust between **Forest B** and **Forest C**, you cannot extend the trust implicitly to a third forest.

To configure forest trust, you need to have forest functional level Windows Server 2003 or newer and DNS name resolution between forests.

Configuring trust filtering

In some scenarios, forest trusts can be a security issue. If a trust is not properly configured, users can gain unwanted access to other forest resources. There are three different types of filtering that can be used to control and prevent potential issues.

- SID filtering
- Selective authentication
- Named suffix routing

SID filtering

When a user authenticates in a trusted domain, the user presents authorization data. This data includes the **Security Identifiers (SIDs)** of all groups that the user belongs to. This data also includes the `SIDHistory` attribute of the user and the user's groups. SID filtering prevents unwanted loads of SIDs from trusted domains by enabling the trusting domain to filter out the SIDs from the trusted domain that are not the primary SIDs of the security principals. SID filtering is enabled by default for all outgoing trusts to external domains and forests.

Selective authentication

When you create a forest trust, you can define the scope of authentication of trusted security principals. It can be either of the following:

- Forest-wide authentication
- Selective authentication

Forest-wide authentication enables all trusted users to authenticate to the trusting domain. If you use this authentication mode, all users from a trusted forest are authenticated users in the trusting domain.

If you choose selective authentication, all users in the trusted domain are trusted identities. They will be allowed to authenticate only for services that you specify. With selective authentication, users will not be part of the authenticated users in the target domain and you need to give them explicit permissions for access.

Named suffix routing

Named suffix routing is a mechanism for managing how authentication requests are routed across forests. By default, AD DS routes unique name suffixes when you create a forest trust. For example, the DNS forest name `mcsacertguide.local` is a unique name suffix in the `mcsacertguide.local` forest. AD DS will route all names that are subordinate to the unique name suffix implicitly. The `uk.mcsacertguide.local` domain will be routed because it is a child domain in the `mcsacertguide.local` forest.

If you want to exclude members of a child domain from authenticating in a specified forest, you need to disable the name suffix routing for that name.

Configuring sites and subnets

AD DS replication within a single site occurs automatically, regardless of the network's utilization. However, if you have different physical locations, which is the most common scenario for multiple sites, utilizing a WAN link can sometimes cause unstable network connectivity. In this scenario, you need to implement different AD DS sites and configure replication and authentication in a proper way. AD DS sites represent physical network infrastructure with objects and provide benefits in multiple locations:

- Management of replication traffic
- Providing service localization
- Linking GPO links directly to the site

The implementation of a subnet object in sites is crucial to the functionality of the site. A subnet object presents logical IP addresses that are assigned to sites and provide correct service localization in a multi-site domain environment. For example, if sites and subnets are properly configured, users from the site will try to authenticate to the domain controllers on site, instead of authenticating with other domain controllers.

Replication between sites is a little bit different to replication within a site. Inter-site replication is compressed to be up to 15% of the original size to optimize network traffic. Replication between sites will occur in a predefined time schedule. The default value is 180 minutes, but the minimum and recommended value is 15 minutes. This schedule can be bypassed in two cases: for account lockout and similar security related changes, as well as for password changes. In this case, replication will occur immediately.

When you have multiple sites, the KCC on one domain controller per site will be promoted to an **Inter-Site Topology Generator** (**ISTG**). The ISTG is responsible for creating the ideal topology for replication based on the configured site links. In some scenarios, you might want to define only specific domain controllers per site, and these will be responsible for inter-site replication. These servers are called **bridgehead servers**. The ISTG will select the bridgehead servers automatically and configure the topology based on these servers, but you can define a bridgehead server manually, if you want.

Creating and configuring site links

A site link is an object that is mandatory for inter-site replication and something that ISTG uses for creating topology. **DEFAULTIPSITELINK** is there by default, but in scenarios where you have three or more sites, this link might be not ideal. **DEFAULTIPSITELINK**, by default, has a cost of 100 and a replication interval of 180 minutes. Although these parameters can be changed, in a scenario in which we have three or more sites, the physical links between those sites are probably not the same, and one site link cannot be appropriate for all sites and their topologies.

In these scenarios, you can create and configure more site links and link the sites to them. Then, you can define the replication interval and the link cost based on the physical network link and your business requirements. For example, if you have three sites – London, New York, and Amsterdam – you can create a dedicated link for London and Amsterdam with a link cost of 20 and a replication interval of 15 minutes, because you have a good link between the sites and locations that need to be replicated as fast as possible. A site link for Amsterdam and New York will also be created and configured with a link cost of 50 and a replication interval of 60 minutes, because we don't need to utilize the network link between these sites in a shorter period of time.

You will then have configured dedicated links between London and Amsterdam, and Amsterdam and New York. In this case, replication between London and New York will not be possible until you create a site link bridge. A site link bridge gives you the possibility to link two or more site links to bypass replication if a dedicated link doesn't exist.

Moving domain controllers between sites

In some scenarios, you will want to move domain controllers between sites. The complete process is easy, and you just need to drag and drop a select domain controller to the desired site using the **Active Directory Sites and Services** MMC Snap-in. ISTG will generate a new topology based on the changes in the sites.

Summary

In this chapter, you have learned how to configure and manage AD in a complex environment. You have also learned how to configure and manage managed service accounts and service principal names, how to configure and manage local and domain passwords and lockout policies, and how to implement and manage AD sites and AD forest and domain trusts.

In next chapter, topic will be Group Policy. You will learn how to implement and manage Group Policies and how to configure applying Group Policy Objects to users and computers.

Questions

1. Is the lockout account policy enabled by default?
   1. Yes
   2. No

2. What is the default time for the replication schedule in **DEFAULTIPSITELINK**?
   1. 15 minutes
   2. 180 minutes
   3. 60 minutes
   4. 150 minutes

3. Fine-grained password policy objects give us the ability to do what?
   1. Configure a more detailed domain password policy
   2. Create a less complex password policy
   3. Create more than one password policy in the domain
   4. Remove an existing password policy and create a new one

4. Which statements to do with authoritative and non-authoritative restoration are correct?
   1. Authoritative restoration can recover only one object
   2. Non-authoritative restoration can recover the whole domain and replicate changes to other domain controllers
   3. Authoritative restoration can replicate recovered objects to other domain controllers
   4. Non-authoritative restoration will be used in case one domain controller fails or gets corrupted

5. Do MSA objects have passwords?
   1. Yes
   2. No

6. What does restartable AD DS allow you to do?
    1. Restart one domain controller at a time
    2. Restart multiple domain controllers at a time
    3. Stop the AD DS service and manage the AD DS database in offline mode
    4. Log in to DSRM and manage the AD DS database

7. To create AD DS database snapshots, which tool do we use?
    1. `Ntdsutil.exe`
    2. `Repadmin.exe`
    3. Active Directory Administrative Center MMC Snap-in
    4. Windows Server Backup

8. If you have three domain controllers on Windows Server 2016 and one on Windows Servers 2012 R2, what is the highest forest level?
    1. Windows Server 2016
    2. Windows Server 2012 R2
    3. Windows Server 2012
    4. Windows Server 2008 R2

9. If you have one domain controller on Windows Server 2016 and three on Windows Servers 2012 R2, what is the highest domain level?
    1. Windows Server 2016
    2. Windows Server 2012 R2
    3. Windows Server 2012
    4. Windows Server 2008 R2

10. If you create a new IP site link, do you need to remove **DEFAULTIPSITELINK**?
    1. Yes
    2. No

Further reading

By going to the following links, you can find more information about the topics that were covered in this chapter:

- **Managed Service Accounts: Understanding, Implementing, Best Practices, and Troubleshooting**: `https://blogs.technet.microsoft.com/askds/2009/09/10/managed-service-accounts-understanding-implementing-best-practices-and-troubleshooting/`

- **Active Directory Forest Trust: attention points**: `https://social.technet.microsoft.com/wiki/contents/articles/50969.active-directory-forest-trust-attention-points.aspx`

- **Setting Up Active Directory Sites, Subnets, and Site-Links**: `https://blogs.technet.microsoft.com/canitpro/2015/03/03/step-by-step-setting-up-active-directory-sites-subnets-site-links/`

- **Backing Up and Restoring an Active Directory Server**: `https://docs.microsoft.com/en-us/windows/desktop/ad/backing-up-and-restoring-an-active-directory-server`

3
Creating and Managing Group Policy

AD DS and Group Policy are among the most useful features in Windows Server operation systems that are used in enterprise environments. From Windows Server 2000, Group Policy is the central administration point for configuring and deploying settings to all computers in an organization. You can define, enforce, and update the entire configuration by using the **Group Policy Object (GPO)** settings, and apply GPOs to the entire organization or to specific users or computers in the organization. Applying GPOs can be filtered based on security group membership and other defined attributes, such as delegation or **Windows Management Instrumentation (WMI)** filters. In this chapter, you'll learn how to implement, configure, and manage Group Policy and GPOs.

We'll cover the following topics in this chapter:

- Creating and managing GPOs
- Understanding Group Policy processing
- Configuring Group Policy settings and preferences

Creating and managing GPOs

In this section, you'll learn what a Group Policy is, how to configure a new GPO, and how to link a GPO to a specific OU. You'll also learn which tools need to be used to create and manage GPOs, and how to back up and restore or copy and import GPOs.

Introduction to Group Policy

Group Policy, as the name implies, is a policy that's applied to a group of objects, such as users or computers. Each policy defines a set of specific configuration parameters that will be applied to AD DS objects. Group Policy is the Microsoft implementation of configuration management and the organization of every enterprise relies on Group Policy. Each GPO is composed of two independent policies, a user and a computer policy, or, in other words, a user configuration and a computer configuration.

These policies can be in three states: Not Configured, Enabled, or Disabled. For group management, you will use two MMC snap-ins: **Group Policy Management** and **Group Policy Management Editor**. Group Policy Management will be used when you want to create or link GPOs, while Group Policy Management Editor is the primary tool used for editing GPOs.

As mentioned, each GPO has two configurations or policies: the computer and the user. Both policies contain only the configuration for a specific type of object, and both are refreshed and applied in periods of 90 to 120 minutes. The computer configuration will be applied whenever an operating system starts, while the user configuration will be applied whenever a user signs in.

In both policies, you can find the following settings:

- **Software Settings**: Contains only the software installation extension
- **Windows Settings**: Contains Windows settings, such as Scripts and Security Settings
- **Administrative Templates**: Contains a large number of settings that can be used to configure the user and computer environment

Managing starter GPOs

Each newly-created GPO is, by default, empty. This gives you the ability to create GPOs based on your needs. Sometimes, you might need to configure more than one GPO with some of the same settings. To avoid repeating the manual steps for each GPO, you can create a starter GPO with preconfigured settings and create a new GPO based on the Starter GPO. Starter GPOs can contain only administrative template settings. You can also export or import starter GPOs from or to another environment. The GPMC stores starter GPOs in a `Starter GPOs` folder, located in `SYSVOL`. 10 Starter GPOs are created by default.

Configuring GPO links

Each GPO you create is stored in a Group Policy Object container. Even if you configure a GPO, it won't be applied to any users or computers in your organization unless you link it to an OU or domain. You can link an existing GPO to an OU, or you can create a new GPO and link it in the same step, as shown here:

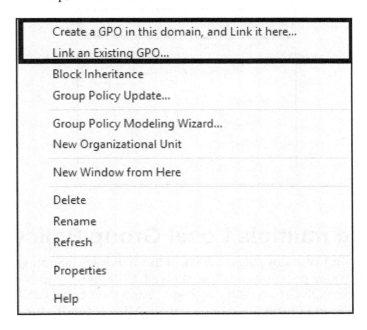

A GPO can be linked to a site, a domain, or an OU. You can link a GPO to more than one site or OU. This is a common scenario and depends on the structure of your OUs. If your OUs are divided based on your location and then based on the object types, such as users or computers, you will most likely have more than one OU with the same object types (such as OU users under OU London, and OU users under OU New York). In this scenario, you need to apply the same GPO to both user OUs. Deleting a GPO link doesn't delete the GPO itself. The GPO will remain in the Group Policy Objects container and the scope of settings will no longer apply to computers and users within the previously-linked container object. The GPO link can also be disabled and the result for the GPO settings applied on an object will be the same as if you had deleted the GPO link.

To disable a GPO link, right-click on it in the GPMC console tree and then clear the **Link Enabled** option. If a link is disabled, you just need to re-enable it, while a deleted link needs to be added again to the specific OU. You can see this option in the following screenshot:

Configuring multiple Local Group Policy

Prior to Windows 7 and Windows Server 2008, in the Windows operating system, only a single Local Group Policy per computer was allowed. With these, you could only manage standalone computers with Group Policy by configuring their Local GPO. With Windows 7, Windows Server 2008, and newer operating systems, Microsoft introduced a feature called Multiple Local GPOs.

The following list shows the types of Local GPOs that are included by default in Windows 7, Windows Server 2008, and newer operating systems:

- At the top is the standard Local Group Policy, which allows you to configure computer-related and user-related settings or policies that apply to all users of a computer, including the Administrator.
- The next layer is the Administrators and Non-Administrators Local Group Policy, which allows you to set polices for users according to which of the two basic groups you have on a standalone computer.
- In the bottom layer is a user-specific Local GPO, which allows you to set policies that apply only to specific users.

Local GPOs can be managed using MMC for Local GPOs and selecting a specific layer of functionality.

Once you start MMC, you just need to add the **Group Policy Object Editor snap-in**, as shown in the following screenshot:

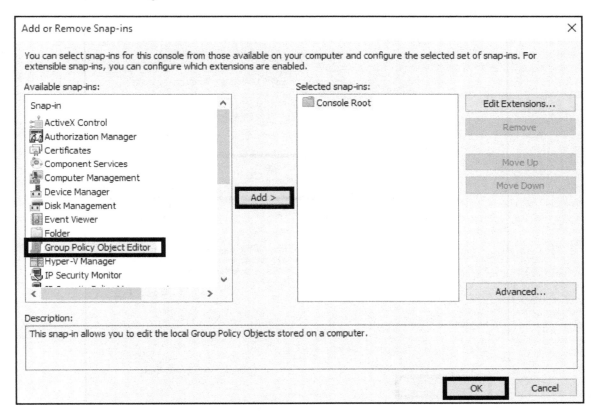

Once you add the Group Policy Object Editor to MMC, you need to open the standard Local GPO or browse to open a more specific Local GPO for a specific user or group:

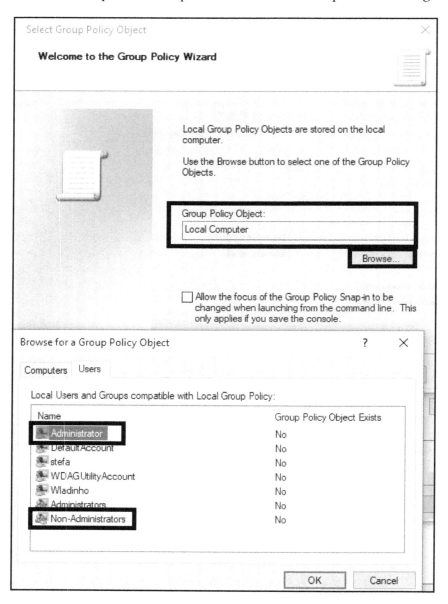

Backing up, importing, copying, and restoring GPOs

Each GPO can be backed up, imported, copied, and restored. These actions are described here:

- **Backing up GPOs**: This is a pretty easy process that you can use to save your GPOs. You can back up GPOs individually or as a whole with the GPMC. Only the backup location needs to be provided, and this can be either a local or a shared location. Every time that you perform a backup, a new backup version of the GPO is created, which provides a historical record.
- **Restoring backed-up GPOs**: If a GPO becomes corrupt or you delete one accidentally, you can restore any of the historical backup versions.

 Restoring a GPO doesn't restore the GPO links. You must do this manually afterward.

- **Importing GPO settings**: If you need a GPO with the same settings as an existing or backed-up GPO, you need to import the GPO settings. The import process consists of two steps: creating a new, empty GPO, and then importing the settings from the backed-up GPO. This can be done in the same domain, as well as in other domains.
- **Copying GPOs**: This operation copies an existing live GPO. A new GPO will be created during this process and get a name in the following format: **Copy of GPOName**.

Resetting default GPOs

Once you install and configure the Active Directory domain, there are two default GPOs: the Default Domain Policy with configured settings about account policies, and the default Domain Controller Policy with settings regarding audit and user rights assignment. Although the best practice for GPOs is not to change anything in these GPOs, some settings can be modified. For example, in the Default Domain Policy, the password, the Kerberos policy, and the account lockout settings can be changed. In the default Domain Controller Policy, you can change settings related to audit policies or to user rights assignment.

In some scenarios, however, these GPOs are changed without plan or are corrupted and you need to restore them to their factory settings. This can be done using the `dcgpofix` command-line tool, but before you run the following commands to restore the default policies to their factory settings, you need to make a backup of the policies.

The command to restore the Default Domain Policy is as follows:

```
dcgpofix /ignoreschema /target:Domain
```

The command to restore the default Domain Controller Policy is as follows:

```
dcgpofix /ignoreschema /target:DC
```

Alternatively, the command to restore both of the default GPOs is as follows:

```
dcgpofix /ignoreschema /target:Both
```

Delegate Group Policy management

In an enterprise environment, you'll probably need to delegate permissions to other users for specific tasks related to the GPO. You can delegate the following Group Policy tasks:

- Creating GPOs
- Editing GPOs
- Managing Group Policy links for a site, domain, or OU
- Performing Group Policy modeling analyses on a given domain or OU
- Reading Group Policy results data for objects in each domain or OU
- Creating WMI filters in a domain

Members of the Domain Admins, Enterprise Admins, and Group Policy Creator Owners groups have full management control over GPOs. The Authenticated Users group has Read and Apply Group Policy permissions for all GPOs. If you want to give someone permission to create GPOs, you can do that in two ways: by adding the user or group to the Group Policy Creator Owners group or by explicitly granting the group or user permission to create GPOs. To edit GPOs, read and write access to the GPO is mandatory. Linking GPOs to a container is a permission that's specific to containers and needs to be provided using permission delegation in the Active Directory Users and Computers MMC snap-in.

Detecting health issues using Group Policy

Like other roles and features on Windows Server, the Group Policy status needs to be checked as a first step in troubleshooting issues with GPO. Although Group Policies are replicated using SYSVOL, which is a stable mechanism, some issues might appear for different reasons. In the Group Policy Object container, under the Group Policy Management editor, you can find a few different tabs where you can check the status of the GPO:

- **Scope**: You can find where the GPO linked to and which security and WMI filters are applied:

- **Details**: This gives you information about the GPO owner, the dates when the GPO was created and modified, the version of the policy, and the GPO status:

- **Settings**: This shows you which settings are configured in the GPO:

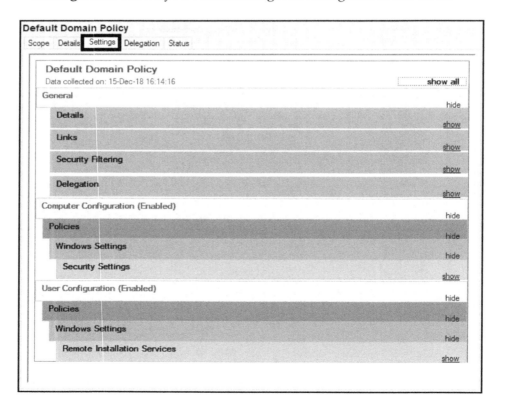

- **Delegation**: This shows the permissions that users or groups have on particular GPOs:

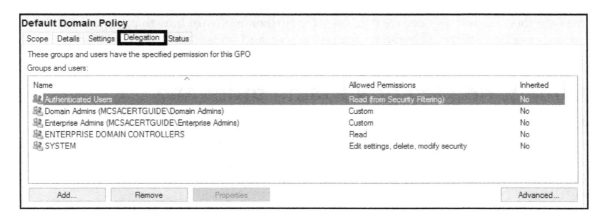

- **Status**: This shows you the status of GPO replication:

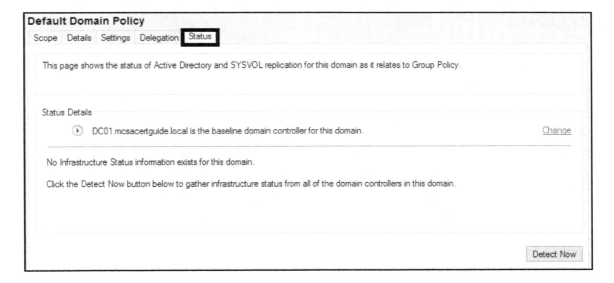

Understanding Group Policy processing

In the previous section, you learned what about Group Policy and how to create and manage them. In this section, we'll go one step further and learn how to configure GPO settings to filter which GPOs can be applied where, and how.

Configuring the processing order and precedence

In a large organization, you might have more than a few GPOs implemented and configured in your environment. If you also have a big AD DS infrastructure and a deep OU hierarchy, understanding Group Policy processing is very important.

As mentioned in the previous section, once created, a GPO isn't enabled and can't be processed until it's linked. GPOs can be linked to sites, domains, OUs, and any nested OUs. By default, GPOs are inherited, which means that GPOs linked to a domain will be processed by all users or computers in all OUs in the domain. Group Policy processing has the following order:

- Local GPOs
- Site-level GPOs
- Domain-level GPOs
- OU GPOs
- Nested OU GPOs

Based on this order, Local GPOs will be processed first, but only for a specific computer. Site-level GPOs will be processed by all objects on a specific site, while domain-level GPOs will affect all objects in a domain. The OU level is the most granular and most common type of Group Policy implementation, because only a specific set of objects will be affected by this setting. For example, the Default Domain Policy, with password and account settings, is linked on the domain level. All the configured settings from this GPO will be applied to all objects in the domain. Domain-level linked GPOs are useful if the configured settings need to be applied to the whole domain, such as WSUS settings or user disclaimers. On an OU level, only GPOs with specific settings for departments or groups of users will be linked and processed.

By default, all GPOs that are directly linked to an OU or inherited from the site, domain, or parent OU, will be processed by objects in that OU. In some scenarios, there might be a lot of GPOs and the situation can become quite confusing. Because of this, it's important to understand the processing and precedence of GPOs.

Each GPO will be processed by an object in a specific OU. This means that a user in the Finance OU, under the Company OU, will process settings from all Local GPOs—site-level and domain-level – as well all GPOs from the parent and OU in which the user is based. If there's no conflict in the GPO's settings, the user will apply all user settings from all inherited GPOs, and all directly-linked GPOs as well. But if there are any conflicts in the user settings in those policies, the user will filter only the conflicted settings and apply the policies that are nearest to the objects. This rule is called **precedence**. A lower precedence number will have a higher priority when settings are applied. By default, the GPO that's linked to the OU first will have the lowest precedence and a higher priority.

If you check the GPO tab called **Group Policy Inheritance**, you'll be able to see the GPO name, precedence, and the location to which the GPOs are linked:

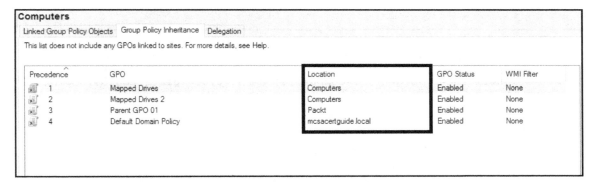

Configuring inheritance blocking

As mentioned, GPOs are, by default, inherited. In some scenarios, however, you might want to disable inheritance for specific OUs. In that case, objects in the OU will only process GPOs that are directly linked to that OU. Nested OUs will have inheritance enabled, but will only be able to inherit GPOs that are directly linked to the parent OU. To enable inheritance blocking using MMC, you need to go to the Group Policy Management console, select the desired OU, and check **Block Inheritance**.

Then, you'll see that only directly-linked GPOs are in the list for that OU:

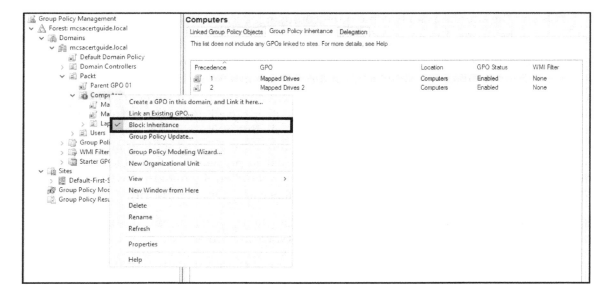

If you want to do this using PowerShell, you need to run the following command:

```
Set-GPinheritance -Target "OU=Computers,OU=Packt,DC=mcsacertguide,DC=local"
-IsBlocked Yes
```

Configuring enforced policies

In contrast to blocking, in some scenarios, you might need to enforce the processing of some GPOs. GPO enforcing will set the highest precedence to that GPO, regardless of their order in the hierarchy. You can do this using MMC Group Policy Management, by selecting desired the GPO and checking **Enforced**, or by using PowerShell:

If you want to do this using PowerShell, you need to run the following command:

```
Set-GPLink -Name "Parent GPO 01" -Target
"OU=Packt,DC=mcsacertguide,DC=local" -Enforced Yes
```

Configuring security filtering and WMI filtering

In the previous section, we mentioned GPO filtering. We will now describe this process in more detail. GPOs can process OUs and all users or computers will be affected by the GPO settings. In some scenarios, you might not want a specific GPO to be processed by all objects. There are two different ways to accomplish this.

By default, all Authenticated Users can read and process settings from GPOs. This is defined in the **Security Filtering** setting in the GPO properties. If you want to isolate a specific user or group to process a specific policy, you just need to remove the Authenticated Users from **Security Filtering** and add the desired user or group, as shown in the following screenshot:

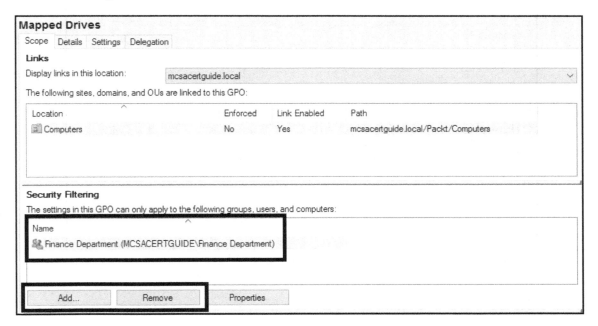

If you want to isolate a specific computer to process a specific GPO, you need to create a WMI filter. A WMI query can filter a system based on its characteristics, such as RAM, CPU, and IP address. WMI queries are written using **WMI Query Language** (**WQL**). For example, if you want to filter only Windows 10 computers, you need to run the following query:

```
select * from Win32_OperatingSystem where Version like "10.%" and
ProductType="1"
```

Before you filter GPO processing with a WMI filter, you need to create a WMI filter. You need to carry out the following steps:

1. Open **MMC Group Policy Management**.
2. Go to **WMI filters**.
3. Create a new WMI filter by adding a filter name, a description, and a query:

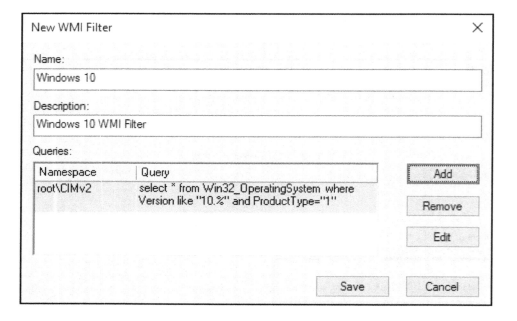

Then, you will be able to select the WMI filter from the drop-down list in the WMI filtering section of the GPO.

Configuring loopback processing

By default, a user will process settings that come from a GPO's user settings based on their OU location. This is the same for computers. In general, this means that users and computers will apply settings from totally different GPOs if they aren't in the same OU. Sometimes, you need to avoid the default option and force the user to process settings from the same GPO as the computer process, regardless of the user's OU. For example, let's say you want all users to have the same settings when they're logged in to computers in a classroom. This can be done with **loopback processing**. This option in Group Policy gives us the ability to bypass the default Group Policy algorithm and force users to apply settings from the same GPO as the computer. Loopback processing is located in the **Computer Configuration** | **Policies** | **Administrative Templates** | **System** | **Group Policy** folder in the Group Policy Management Editor. It can be set to **Not Configured**, **Enabled**, or **Disabled**. Once you enable it, you can choose between one of two modes:

- **Replace**: This replaces the GPO user settings entirely with the GPO that has already been obtained for the computer.
- **Merge**: This applies user settings from the GPO that the user processes by default. If there are any conflicts in the settings, the user settings from the GPO that the computer obtains during startup will have a higher precedence.

In the following screenshot, you can see the GPO setting that needs to be configured in order to enable the loopback processing mode:

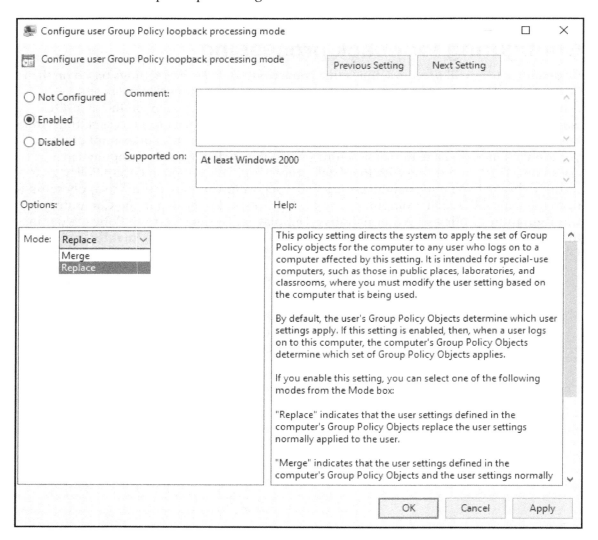

Configuring Group Policy caching

One of the most important concepts in terms of Group Policy is how clients process GPOs. It's really important to understand that applying GPO settings is a completely client-based task. On Windows Vista, Windows 2008, and later, the Group Policy Client is responsible for retrieving the GPOs from the domain. Once downloaded, GPOs are cached locally. The Group Policy Client then triggers a **Client-Side Extension (CSE)** that is responsible for applying the settings from GPOs. By default, the CSE will reapply the settings from only the GPOs that are changed, but the CSE can also be configured to reapply settings from all GPOs, regardless of whether or not they have changed. The CSE will also reapply security settings from GPOs every 16 hours, even if the settings aren't changed.

CSE can be reconfigured to reapply settings even if GPOs aren't changed by changing the **Registry Policy Processing** for the **Registry CSE** in **Computer Configuration** | **Policies** | **Administrative Templates** | **System** | **Group Policy.** You need to click **Enable** and select **Process even if the Group Policy objects have not changed**.

Forcing a Group Policy update

As mentioned earlier in this chapter, GPOs are updated in intervals of 90 to 120 minutes. Sometimes, you need to apply new settings immediately and you don't want to check the next period to apply the GPO. One way to do this is to invoke an update on the GPOs locally. You can run one of two possible commands locally on the computer—if you're using the Command Prompt, you need to run the gpudate /force command. If you're using PowerShell, you need to run Invoke-GPUpdate. Although these commands are enough in most scenarios, some situations require you to invoke an update on the GPOs to all, or a specific set of, computers. From Windows Server 2012, you're now able to refresh GPOs remotely. Administrators can use the Group Policy Management console and the target OU and force Group Policy updates. This can be done within 10 minutes.

Configuring Group Policy settings and preferences

In general, Group Policy is divided into two sets of settings that can be used to configure user and computer settings in domain environments: Administrative templates and Group Policy preferences. Administrative templates, also known as registry-based policies, provide most of the available GPO settings that modify specific registry keys. Registry-based policies are the simplest and best way to support the centralized management of policy settings. Group Policy preferences can, in general, be substituted by implementing scripts to configure settings. From Windows Server 2008, Group Policy preferences are part of Group Policies and allow you to deliver a lot of common settings, such as mapped drivers, printers, and registry changes.

In this section, you'll learn how to configure Administrative templates and Group Policy preference settings for users and computers.

Defining network drive mappings

One of the most common settings that needs to be configured with Group Policy is mapping network drive.

Many users in business environments use file servers to store business data, but for most of them access to data through the **Universal Naming Convention** (UNC) path is very complicated. Configuring a mapped drive solves this problem because users will access this data in a similar way as they access local drives.

In Windows Server 2016, you can do this using GPO in two different ways. One of these ways is to create a script and configure it to run when a computer starts up or when a user logs in. This approach is not necessary in most scenarios, because Group Policy preferences include settings for Drive Maps. You can find these settings under **User Configuration** | **Preferences** | **Windows Settings** | **Drive Maps**:

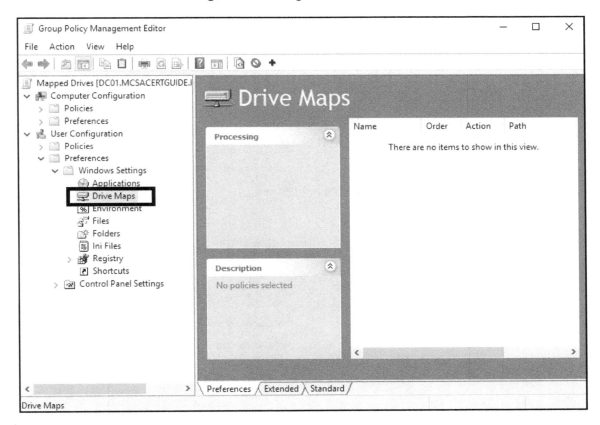

Once you open this setting, you can create a new mapped drive and apply it to users. Like every other Group Policy preference, you can **Create**, **Update**, **Delete**, and **Replace** settings in the GPO. The following example shows you one of the possible options for configuring Drive Maps using Group Policy preferences:

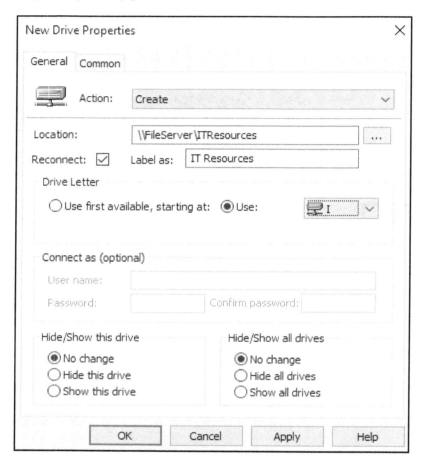

Configuring custom registry settings

Like Drive Maps, many custom registry settings can also be deployed with Group Policy, using one of the Group Policy preference settings. You can find these settings under **User Configuration** I **Preferences** I **Windows Settings** I **Registry**. Registry settings can be configured using one of the three options for configuration, **Registry Item**, **Collection Item**, and **Registry Wizard**, which are described here:

- A Registry Item allows you to manually change single entries.
- A Collection Item allows you to organize registry preference items into a folder.
- The Registry Wizard allows you to use the local machine, as well as a remote machine.

In the following screenshot, you can see where the registry settings can be found in GPO:

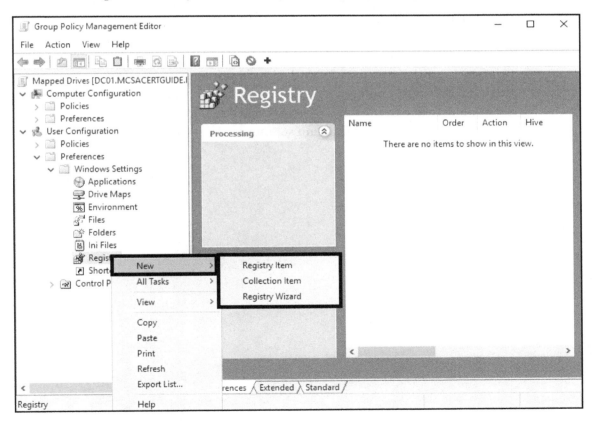

Configuring the Control Panel settings

Control Panel settings are also important for configuring users' computers. In the Group Policy preferences, settings related to mapped drives or the registry are part of Windows Settings. The other section in Group Policy preferences is Control Panel settings, where you can find a lot of other settings, including the following:

- **Data Source**: Defines the data source
- **Device**: Configures the device class and type
- **Folder Options**: Configures the folder options for Windows XP or Vista, and newer OSes
- **Internet Settings**: Configures the basic Internet Explorer settings for versions 5 to 10
- **Local Users and Groups**: Configures local users or groups on computers
- **Network Options**: Configures VPN or dial-in connections
- **Power Options**: Configures power options or schemes for XP, or power plans for Windows 7 and newer operating systems
- **Printers**: Configures shared, TCP/IP, or local printers
- **Regional Settings**: Configures regional options
- **Scheduled Tasks**: Creates and manages scheduled tasks
- **Start Menu**: Configures start menu settings for Windows XP or Vista, and newer operating systems

The following screenshot shows the preceding settings:

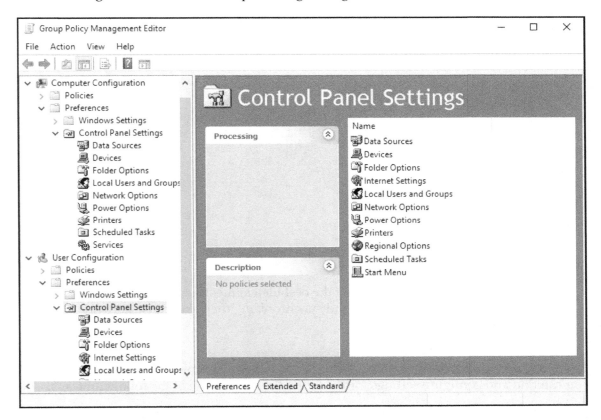

Configuring folder redirections

This Group Policy feature is useful in many different scenarios. Folder redirection allows you to configure user folders to be located at a network location and still appear as a local folder. With this feature, you can ensure that users can access their data, regardless of the computer they are signed in on. **Folder Redirection** supports Offline File technology for synchronization, which ensures that users have access to their data even if they don't have network access.

The following folders can be redirected:

- AppData(Roaming)
- Contacts
- Desktop
- Documents
- Downloads
- Favorites
- Links
- Music
- Pictures
- Saved Games
- Searches
- Start Menu
- Videos

 Redirecting all folders isn't the best idea in most scenarios. Some folders can take a lot of storage, and synchronizing them can cause network congestion.

In GPO, under **User Configuration** | **Policies** | **Windows Settings** | **Folder Redirection**, you can find and configure settings for Folder Redirection in one of the following ways:

- **None**: This is the default setting and means that **Folder Redirection** is not enabled.
- **Basic**: This means folders are redirected for all users to the same location.
- **Advanced**: This means that the location for redirection can vary based on security groups.

If you decide to use **Basic** or **Advanced** settings, you need to know that each user will have their own redirected folder under the root path, regardless of what type of redirection you've selected. Also, the configuration for folder redirection might be different for each folder that can be redirected, meaning you don't need to redirect all user folders.

The following screenshot shows where you can find the **Folder Redirection** setting in GPO:

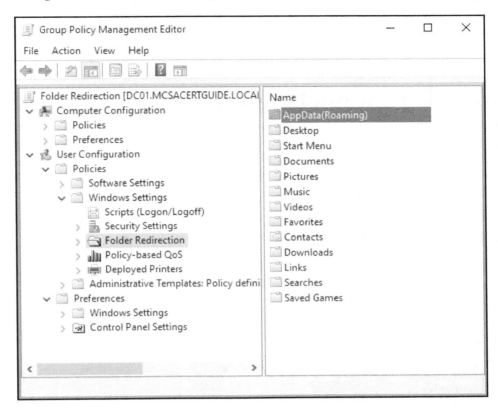

Security permissions for redirected folders are configured by default. Although it isn't recommended to do so, you can change these permissions as follows:

- **NTFS permissions for the root folder:**
  - **Administrator**: None
  - **Security group of users that save data on the root shared folder**: List Folder, Create Folders
  - **System**: Full Control
- **Share permissions for root folder:**
  - **Security group of users that save data on the root shared folder**: Full Control

- **NTFS permissions for a user's redirected folder:**
    - **%Username%**: Full Control, owner of folder
    - **Administrators**: Full Control
    - **System**: Full Control

Configuring shortcut deployment

How many times have you encountered a situation where you need to configure some type of shortcut for users? For example, this might be the case if you've implemented a new internal site or web application but the users aren't aware because they expect to see a shortcut in their desktops. In this case, you can use GPOs to create and configure a desired shortcut and deploy it with Group Policy.

This configuration is part of Group Policy preferences and you can find it under **User Configuration** | **Preferences** | **Windows Settings** | **Shortcut**:

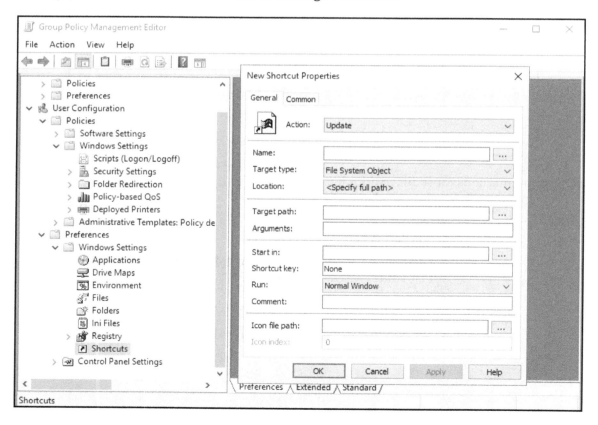

With these settings, you can create and configure a shortcut in the same way as on a local computer. You first need to define the type of shortcut, the target, and where will be stored. Once configured, the shortcut will be available for users after the Group Policy is applied for the first time.

Configuring item-level targeting

One of the features of Group Policy preferences is item-level targeting. This feature allows you to configure Group Policy preferences with some condition types and make targeting more detailed. Item-level targeting has 27 different categories for user and computer objects, all of which can be combined with **AND** or **OR** parameters. Item-level targeting is refreshable and users or computers that are aligned later with conditions will process GPOs during the refresh interval.

Each Group Policy preference on the properties page has a **Common** tab, where you can find **Item-level targeting**:

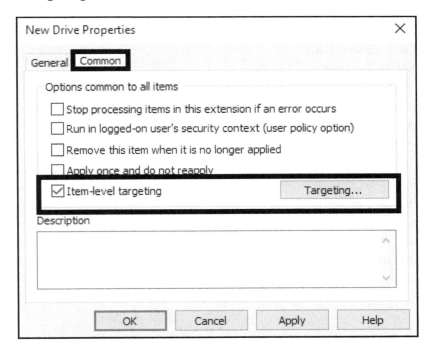

Item-level targeting contains the following categories:

- **Battery Present**
- **Computer Name**
- **CPU Speed**
- **Date Match**
- **Disk Space**
- **Domain**
- **Environment Variable**
- **File Match**
- **IP Address Range**
- **Language**
- **LDAP Query**
- **MAC Address Range**
- **MSI Query**
- **Network Connection**
- **Operating System**
- **Organizational Unit**
- **PCMCIA Present**
- **Portable Computer**
- **Processing Mode**
- **RAM**
- **Registry Match**
- **Security Group**
- **Site**
- **Terminal Session**
- **Time Range**
- **User**
- **WMI Query**

These categories can be seen in the following screenshot:

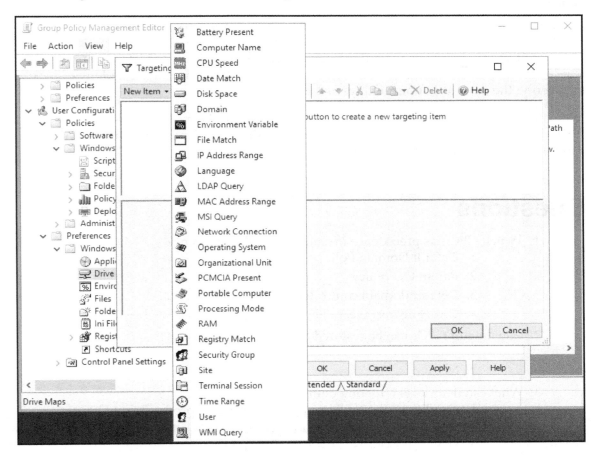

You might need to implement item-level targeting in a range of different scenarios, including the following:

- Processing GPOs for computers in specified networks
- Mapping network drives depending on security group membership
- Applying setting to computers based on the OS

Summary

In this chapter, you learned about the most important components of Group Policy. You also learned the purpose of Group Policies and how to configure and implement them. Group Policies can help you to configure a lot of different settings on user or computer objects, but due to the quantity of settings that can be configured, in this chapter we stuck to covering the most important settings and concepts.

In the next chapter, we'll cover various concepts to do with **Public Key Infrastructure (PKI)**, including how to install and manage **Active Directory Certificate Services** (AD CS) and how to manage a Certification Authority and certificates.

Questions

1. Which GPO has precedence in standard GPO processing?
   1. Default Domain Policy
   2. Parent OU policy
   3. Default domain controller policy
   4. Object nearest OU policy
2. Can default GPOs can be restored to their original state?
   1. Yes
   2. No
3. What can item-level targeting define?
   1. Conditions that will be applied during the processing of GPOs
   2. Number of objects that can apply the same policy
   3. Network speed needed to process GPOs
   4. Additional rules to successfully apply GPOs
4. What are the two modes of loopback processing?
   1. Merge and Remove
   2. Replace and Create
   3. Create and Remove
   4. Merge and Replace

5. Can a backed-up GPO be restored on another domain?
   1. Yes
   2. No

6. Can GPOs be copied to another domain?
   1. Yes
   2. No

7. Which PowerShell cmdlet needs to be used to configure blocking inheritance?
   1. `Set-GPOBlock`
   2. `Set-GPInherintace`
   3. `New-GPOBlock`
   4. `Set-GPORule`

8. In which situation would we use WMI Filters?
   1. Filtering GPOs applying based on OUs
   2. Filtering GPOs applying based on computer hardware or software
   3. Configuring permissions for GPOs
   4. Adding additional layers to GPO authentication

Further reading

Check out the following links for more information about Group Policies:

- `https://blogs.technet.microsoft.com/musings_of_a_technical_tam/2012/02/13/group-policy-basics-part-1-understanding-the-structure-of-a-group-policy-object/`
- `https://blogs.technet.microsoft.com/musings_of_a_technical_tam/2012/02/15/group-policy-basics-part-2-understanding-which-gpos-to-apply/`

4
Understanding and Implementing Active Directory Certificate Services

Nowadays, security is the most critical part of every IT infrastructure and organization. By implementing **Public Key Infrastructure** (**PKI**), you can solve many common security issues. By default, Windows Server can offer Certification Authority as a Windows Server role, and then all you need to do is implement and manage that role. In this chapter, you will learn how to install, configure, and manage CA roles in Windows Server 2016.

We will cover the following topics:

- Installing and configuring AD CS
- Managing certificates and templates
- Managing AD CS

Installing and configuring AD CS

This section will cover the installation and configuration of **Certification Authority** (**CA**), an important part of Microsoft PKI. You will learn how to install and configure Enterprise-integrated and Standalone CAs, and how to manage them.

An overview of AD CS

Active Directory Certification Services (**AD CS**) allows you to implement PKI, so you can easily issue and manage certificates in the Windows Server infrastructure to meet organizational requirements. PKI is a set of software, technologies, encryption, and processes that enables organization to secure communications and transactions. PKI relies on certificate exchange between authenticated users and services. In the Windows Server environment, you can design PKI by implementing AD CS to meet the following security requirements:

- **Confidentiality**: Encrypting data using an Encrypting File System or encrypting network traffic using IPSec
- **Integrity**: Digitally signing data by using AD CS certificates
- **Authenticity**: Using hash algorithms
- **Non-repudiation**: Digitally signing data with the author's certificate
- **Availability**: Installing multiple CA servers in your organization

AD CS in Windows Server 2016 comes with a few role services that can either work together or separately:

- **Certification Authority (CA)**: The main responsibility of the CA is to issue and revoke certificates and to publish **authority information access** (**AIA**) and revocation information. By installing a CA in your organization, you will have established PKI. You can install more than one CA, but only one can be a root CA, with the highest position in the hierarchy.
- **Certification Authority Web Enrollment**: Provides a mechanism for non-domain users, computers, and devices to enroll and renew certificates.
- **Online Responder**: This component can be used for configuring and managing **Online Certificate Status Protocol** (**OCSP**) validation and revocation checking.
- **Network Device Enrollment Service (NDES)**: Provides a mechanism for obtaining certificates for network devices.
- **Certificate Enrollment Web Service (CES)**: Works as a proxy client between a computer that is not domain-joined and that is running Windows 7 or later and CA.
- **Certificate Enrollment Policy Web Service**: Enables users to obtain certificate enrollment policy information. In cooperation with CES, it enables policy-based certificate enrollment when a computer is not domain-joined.

As mentioned, AD CS can either be installed as a single server, or it can be installed in one of many different hierarchy models. Although it is not mandatory to have more than one CA installed in an organization, most small organizations implement a hierarchy based on one server. The best practice is, of course, having at least two CAs. A multi-level hierarchy is more appropriate for larger organizations.

In general, CA hierarchies are separated into a few categories:

- **Policy CA hierarchy**: In this scenario, a subordinate CA is directly below the root CA. The root CA will issue a certificate to the subordinate CA, which will then issue certificates only to other CAs.
- **Cross-certification trust**: Two independent CA hierarchies interoperate when a CA in one hierarchy issues a cross-certified CA certificate to a CA in another hierarchy. You need to have established trust between the CA hierarchies.
- **Two-tier hierarchy**: There is a root CA with least one subordinate CA. The subordinate CA is responsible for policies and issuing certificates to users and computers.

AD CS can be deployed either as an Enterprise-integrated or a Standalone CA. This doesn't depend on the hierarchy, as just the functionality and the configuration are different. Enterprise-integrated AC DS relies on AD DS and has some benefits, such as auto-enrollment, while Standalone AD CS doesn't need AD DS and doesn't have all the functionalities of Enterprise AD CS.

Installing Active Directory Integrated Enterprise Certificate Authority

The AD CS installation process is almost the same as the installation process of other roles. You can do this either by using the Server Manager console or by using PowerShell. Before you start the installation process, you need to make sure you know the following information:

- Computer name and domain membership
- Standalone or Enterprise CA
- Validity period
- CSP, hash algorithm, and key character length

The computer name and the domain membership cannot be changed once AD CS is installed.

Once you collect all the necessary information, you can start by installing and configuring the AD CS role and CA on Windows Server 2016. Like AD DS, the role first needs to be installed:

1. Open **Server Manager** and go to **Add Roles and Features**.
2. On the **Server Roles** page, check **Active Directory Certificate Services**, click **Add Features**, and then click **Next**.
3. On **Features**, click **Next**.
4. On the **AD CS** page, click **Next**.
5. On the **Role Services** page, check all role services that you want to install.
6. On the **Confirmation** page, click **Install**.

Depending on the selected role services, more pages can be shown during the installation process.

If you want to install AD CS with all the role services using PowerShell, you need to run the following command:

```
Install-WindowsFeature AD-Certificate -IncludeAllSubFeature -
IncludeManagementTools
```

Depends on the role service that you want to install, PowerShell commands can vary. If you want to install only some of the role services, you need to use the following role service names in the PowerShell command instead of AD-Certificate:

Certification Authority	ADCS-Cert-Authority
Certificate Enrollment Policy Web Service	ADCS-Enroll-Web-Pol
Certificate Enrollment Web Service	ADCS-Enroll-Web-Svc
Certification Authority Web Enrollment	ADCS-Web-Enrollment
Network Device Enrollment Service	ADCS-Device-Enrollment
Online Responder	ADCS-Online-Cert

Once you have installed AD CS with some or all of the role services, you need to configure the CA:

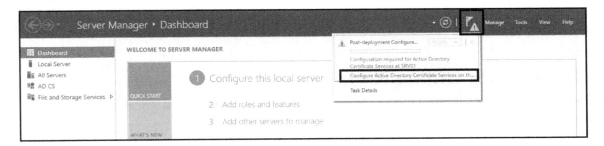

You can do this using the Server Manager console by performing Post-deployment Configuration, following these steps:

1. On the **Credentials** page, define the credentials that will be used during configuration.
2. On the **Role Services** page, check the role services that are installed and need to be configured.
3. On the **Server Type** page, select **Enterprise CA**.
4. On the **CA Type** page, select **Root CA**.
5. On the **Private key** page, select **Create a new private key**.
6. On the **Cryptography** page, specify the cryptographic options.
7. On the **CA Name** page, specify the name of the CA.
8. On the **Validity period** page, specify the validity period.
9. On the **Certificate Database** page, specify the database location.
10. On the **Confirmation** page, click **Configure**.

If you want to configure CA using PowerShell, you need to run the following command:

```
Install-AdcsCertificationAuthority -CAType EnterpriseRootCa -CACommonName
MCSA-CA -CryptoProviderName "RSA#Microsoft Software Key Storage Provider" -
KeyLength 2048 -HashAlgorithmName SHA1 -ValidityPeriod Years -
ValidityPeriodUnits 3
```

For more information regarding the installation and configuration of AD CS role services, please use the following link:

https://docs.microsoft.com/en-us/powershell/module/adcsdeployment/?view=win10-ps

Installing offline roots and subordinate CAs

As mentioned earlier, one of the AD CS deployment types based on hierarchy is installing the offline root CA and at least one subordinate CA. This hierarchy type is called two-tier hierarchy. In this scenario, you need to set up two separated CAs and then configure them.

Configuring Offline Root CA

The installation process is the same as for Enterprise CA, but the configuration is different. You need to follow these steps:

1. On the **Credentials** page, define the credentials that will be used during configuration.
2. On the **Role Services** page, check that the role services are installed and need to be configured.
3. On the **Server Type** page, select **Standalone CA**.
4. On the **CA Type** page, select **Root CA**.
5. On the **Private key** page, select **Create a new private key**.
6. On the **Cryptography** page, specify the cryptographic options.
7. On the **CA Name** page, specify the name of the CA.
8. On the **Validity period** page, specify the validity period.
9. On the **Certificate Database** page, specify the database location.
10. On the **Confirmation** page, click **Configure**.

Although the offline CA can be a domain member, installing it on a server that is a domain member can cause problems with a secure channel. It is highly recommended to install the offline root on a standalone machine as a Standalone CA.

The PowerShell command that needs to be used to configure the Standalone Root CA is as follows:

```
Install-AdcsCertificationAuthority -CAType StandaloneRootCA -CACommonName
Offline-Root-CA -CryptoProviderName "RSA#Microsoft Software Key Storage
Provider" -KeyLength 2048 -HashAlgorithmName SHA1 -ValidityPeriod Years -
ValidityPeriodUnits 3
```

Once you have installed and configured Standalone Root CA, you need to carry out further configuration to prepare your environment to use it. Because offline root CA is designed to be offline, you need to configure a new location for **Certification Revocation List (CRL)** and AIA. To change these settings, you need to follow these steps:

1. Open the **Certificate Authority** console.
2. Right-click on the CA server name and select **Properties**.
3. Select the **Extensions** tab.
4. Click on **Add...** for the **CRL Distribution Point (CDP)** extension:

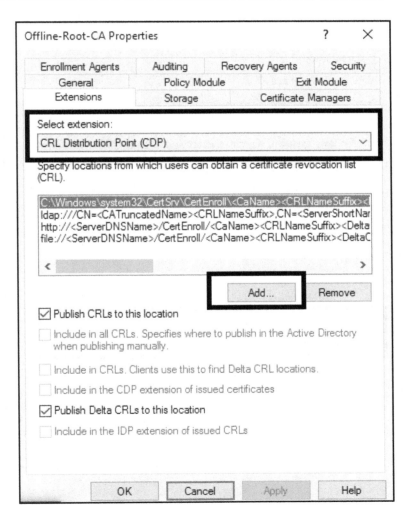

5. In **Location**, add
   file://\\SubortinateFQDN\CertData\<CaName><CRLNameSuffix>
   <DeltaCRLAllowed>.crl and click **OK**.
6. Check the **Include in the CDP extension of issued certificates** and **Include in CRLs. Clients use this to find Delta CRL locations** checkboxes and click **Apply**:

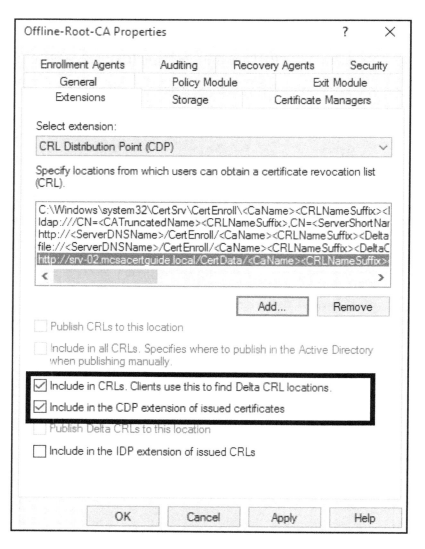

7. In the **Select Extension** drop-down menu, select **Authority Information Access (AIA)** and click **Add**:

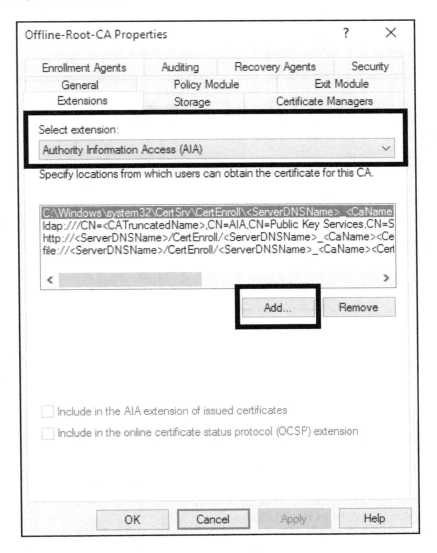

8. In **Location**, add
   file://\\SubordinateFQDN\CertData\<ServerDNSName>_<CaName><Certificat eName>.crt and click **OK**.
9. Check the **Include in the AIA extension of issued certificates** checkbox, click **OK**, and select **Yes** to restart the AD CS service.

Once you have changed the CDP and AIA locations, you need to export the root certificate to **DER encoded binary X.509 (.CER)** format and copy it to the subordinate CA. You need to copy files from `C:\Windows\System32\CertSrv\CertEnroll` to the Subordinate CA.

You need to open the properties of the Offline Root CA and export the certificate, as shown in this screenshot:

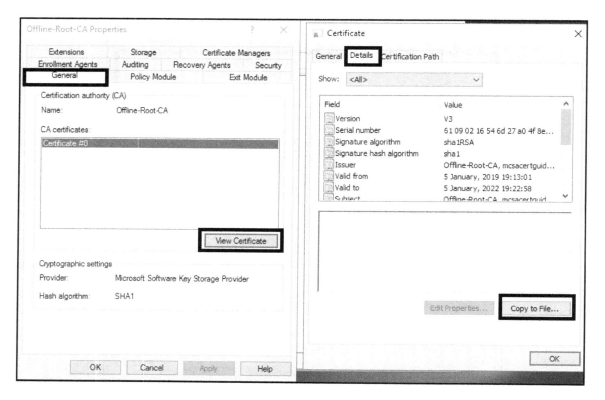

The shared folder needs to be created and configured in the Subordinate CA prior to re-configuring the CDP and AIA locations; otherwise, you will get some errors. Also, the Offline Root CA server needs to have valid DNS A record in the DNS zone.

If you have any issues with publishing the CRL to a shared location on another computer, the following link might be useful: `https://social.technet.microsoft.com/wiki/contents/articles/3081.ad-cs-error-the-directory-name-is-invalid-0x8007010b-win32http-267.aspx`

Configuring the subordinate CA

The process of installing the Enterprise Subordinate CA is the same as all other CA installation processes; it can be done either using the Server Manager console or by using PowerShell. The configuration is different, as shown in these steps:

1. On the **Credentials** page, define credentials that will be used during configuration.
2. On the **Role Services** page, check the role services that are installed and need to be configured.
3. On the **Server Type** page, select **Enterprise CA**.
4. On the **CA Type** page, select **Subordinate CA**.
5. On the **Private key** page, select **Create a new private key**.
6. On the **Cryptography** page, specify the cryptographic options.
7. On the **CA Name** page, specify the name of the CA.
8. On the **Certificate Request** page, select **Save a certificate request to file on the target machine** and specify the location.
9. On the **Certificate Database** page, specify the database location.
10. On the **Confirmation** page, click **Configure**.

The PowerShell command for configuration is as follows:

```
Install-AdcsCertificationAuthority -CAType EnterpriseSubordinateCA -
CACommonName Subordinate-CA -CryptoProviderName "RSA#Microsoft Software Key
Storage Provider" -KeyLength 2048 -HashAlgorithmName SHA1 -
OutputCertRequestFile C:\SRV02.mcsacertguide.local_mcsacertguide-SRV02-
CA.req
```

After that, you need to install the root certificate in **Trusted Root Certification Authorities**, which was previously exported from the Offline Root CA server. All files that are copied from C:\Windows\System32\CertSrv\CertEnroll need to be moved to a shared folder that was previously created and configured as a CDP and AIA location.

The last step in configuring Subordinate CA is to obtain a valid certificate from root CA by using the previously created certificate request file. To do this, you need to perform the following steps on the root CA:

1. Open **Certificate Authority**.
2. Right-click on the root CA server, click on **All tasks**, and select **Submit new request**.
3. Click on **Pending Request**, right-click on certificate, click **All tasks**, and select **Issue**.

If you don't see any certificates in the pending folder, you need to refresh the CA console.

After 15 to 20 seconds, the certificate will be issued to the subordinate CA. As a final step, you need to export the issued certificate in **PKCS #7 Certificates (.P7B)** format with the **Include all certificates in the certification path if possible** option selected. The exported certificate needs to be copied to Subordinate CA and installed using the CA console. Here are the steps:

1. Open the **Certificate Authority** console.
2. Right click on Subordinate CA, click on **All tasks**, and select **Install CA certificate**.
3. Select the certificate that has been exported and copied from root CA and click **Open**.

After 20 to 30 seconds, Subordinate CA will be up and running.

Installing Standalone CAs

The process of installing and configuring Standalone CAs is similar to other installations, but differs with regard to the configuration steps. Once you have installed the desired AD CS role services, you can configure a Standalone CA as follows:

1. On the **Credentials** page, define the credentials that will be used during configuration.
2. On the **Role Services** page, check the role services that are installed and need to be configured.
3. On the **Server Type** page, select **Standalone CA**.
4. On the **CA Type** page, select **Root CA**.
5. On the **Private key** page, select **Create a new private key**.
6. On the **Cryptography** page, specify the cryptographic options.
7. On the **CA Name** page, specify the name of the CA.
8. On the **Validity period** page, specify the validity period.
9. On the **Certificate Database** page, specify the database location.
10. On the **Confirmation** page, click **Configure**.

The PowerShell command that needs to be used to configure the Standalone Root CA is as follows:

```
Install-AdcsCertificationAuthority -CAType StandaloneRootCA -CACommonName
StandaloneRoot-CA -CryptoProviderName "RSA#Microsoft Software Key Storage
Provider" -KeyLength 2048 -HashAlgorithmName SHA1 -ValidityPeriod Years -
ValidityPeriodUnits 3
```

Configuring Certificate Revocation List (CRL) distribution points

To ensure that the PKI infrastructure functions properly, you must configure **CRL Distribution Points (CDPs)** and AIA extensions for each CA:

- AIA addresses are the URLs that tell a certificate verifier the location of the CA certificate.
- CDP addresses are the URLs that tell a certificate verifier the location of the CRL that the CA maintains.

Each issued certificate contains the AIA and CDP URLs that you configured on the CA, at the time the CA issued the certificate. At least one URL needs to be accessible or the verifier will recognize the certificate as invalid.

 AIA and CDP URLs locations can be HTTP, **File Transfer Protocol (FTP)**, **Lightweight Directory Access Protocol (LDAP)**, or file addresses.

If you have implemented Enterprise CA, both extension's values are automatically configured and stored in AD DS. CA certificates and CRLs are available in the AD DS configuration partition and will be replicated to all domain controllers in the AD DS forest. If you want to deploy an offline or a Standalone CA, you need to be aware that extensions and values need to be populated manually, because neither CA implementation will be part of AD DS. The strings that need to be used to configure CDP are as follows: `file://\\ServerFQDN\CertData\<CaName><CRLNameSuffix>;<DeltaCRLAllowed>.crl` or
`http://ServerFQDN/CertData/<CaName><CRLNameSuffix><DeltaCRLAllowed>.crl`
.

To configure AIA, the strings need to be as follows:
```
file://\\ServerFQDN\CertData\<ServerDNSName>_<CaName><CertificateName>.
crt or
http://ServerFQDN/CertData/<ServerDNSName>_<CaName><CertificateName>.cr
t.
```

 In the *Configuring Offline Root CA* section, we described the process of changing extension values step by step.

Installing and configuring Online Responder

Online Responder is a role service in AD CS that provides a more effective way to check the CRL status. By using **Online Certificate Status Protocol (OCSP)**, Online Responder submits certificate status requests using HTTP. The Online Responder service searches CRLs dynamically for the clients and informs them about the certificate status. You should implement Online Responder on a different computer than CA and configure CA to include the URL of the Online Responder in the AIA extension:

1. Open the **Certificate Authority** console.
2. Right-click on the CA server name and select **Properties**.
3. Select the **Extensions** tab.
4. In the **Select Extension** drop-down menu, select **Authority Information Access (AIA)** and click **Add**.
5. In **Location**, add `http://OnlineResponderServerFQDN/ocsp` and click **OK**.
6. Check the **Include in the online certificate status protocol (OCSP) extension** checkbox, click **OK** and select **Yes** to restart the AD CS service.

Then, you need to configure the OCSP Signing certificate so that it can be issued, using the CA console:

1. Open **Certificate Authority**.
2. Right-click on **Certificate Templates**, click **New**, and select **Certificate Template to Issue**.
3. Select **OCSP Response Signing** and click **OK**.

Before selecting the OCPS Response Signing certificate to issue, you need to add the computer account of the Online Responder server to the security properties of the certificate with enroll and auto-enroll permissions.

On the Online Responder server, you need to install the AD CS role service. This can be done using the Server Manager console or the following PowerShell command:

```
Install-WindowsFeature ADCS-Online-Cert -IncludeAllSubFeature -
IncludeManagementTools
```

Once installed, the Online Responder role service needs to be configured. The initial configuration just needs to confirm the installation, and this can be done using the Server Manager console by performing post-install configuration or using the following PowerShell command:

```
Install-AdcsOnlineResponder -Force
```

After the initial configuration, you need to perform a more detailed configuration using the Online Responder Management console:

1. Open the **Online Responder Management** console.
2. Right-click on **Revocation Configuration** and select **Add Revocation Configuration**.
3. On the **Name the Revocation Configuration** page, specify the name of the configuration.
4. On the **Select CA Certificate Location** page, select **Select a certificate for an existing Enterprise CA**.
5. On the **Choose CA Certificate** page, select **Browse CA certificates published in Active Directory**, click on **Browse,** and select **root certificate**.
6. On the **Selecting Signing Certificate** page, select **Automatically select a signing certificate** and click on **Next**.
7. On the **Revocation Provider** page, click on **Finish**.

After these steps, your Online Responder is configured and ready for use. Now, if you enroll a new certificate, for example for a client, you will see in the certificate properties that Online Responder and OCSP are configured:

Implementing administrative role separation

AD CS fully supports **Role-Based Access Control (RBAC)**, but these roles are not created by default. RBAC provides the ability to delegate permissions to specific groups, instead of users, to minimize administrative effort and permission delegation. Each role that you create should only be able to perform a predetermined task or group of tasks. You should plan and create only the roles that are necessary for your organization and then assign appropriate permissions to AD CS.

Configuring CA backup and recovery

As mentioned earlier, AD CS is a service that is usually intended to work for many years. However, over the years, you will probably need to update the hardware or upgrade the operating systems on machines where CA is installed. CA, unfortunately, is not an application that you can just install on a new machine. If you want to move CA to a new computer, the most important thing is to keep the identity. If the CA identity is not retained during the migration to a new server, you may be in trouble because the identity of the issued certificates will not be valid. This can directly affect all processes that rely on certificates, such as file encryption. The procedure of moving is separated into two phases:

- Backing up CA
- Restoring CA

Backing up CA

The backup procedure consists of the following steps:

1. Record the names of the certificate templates. All the names are in AD DS, so you don't need to back them up.
2. Back up the CA using the CA Backup Wizard. You need to back up the private key and the CA certificate, as well as the certificate database and the certificate database log.
3. Export the following registry subkey: `HKEY_LOCAL_MACHINE\SYSTEM\CurrentControlSet\Services\CertSvc\Configuration`.
4. Uninstall the CA from the old server, and then rename the old server or permanently disconnect it from the network.

Restoring CA

Restoring the CA procedure consists of the following steps:

1. Install AD CS with the same role services and in the same deployment scenario as the removed server.
2. Don't create a new certificate. Use the exported private key from the old server.
3. Define the database location, the same as on the old server.
4. After installing the new CA server, open the CA console and stop the AD CS service.
5. Restore the exported registry subkeys.
6. Restore the CA configuration using the CA console.
7. Once the restoration is complete, restart the AD CS service.
8. If you restored Enterprise CA, restore the certificate templates that were previously recorded.

Managing certificates and templates

Once installed, AD CS is ready to issue certificates to computers and users. In this section, you will learn how to manage certificates and templates.

Managing certificates

As mentioned earlier, a certificate is a file that contains information about its owner, such as their email address, their name, the certificate usage type, and AIA and CDP URLs. All of this information will be issued from the certificate template. Each certificate also has a pair of keys, private, and public keys, which will be used in the processes of digital signing, identity validation, and encryption. The pair of keys works in the following ways:

- Content that is encrypted with the public key can be decrypted only with the private key.
- Content that is encrypted with the private key can be decrypted only with the public key.
- Only the keys from a single pair of keys work with each other.
- The private key cannot be derived in a reasonable amount of time from a public key, and vice versa.

During the enrollment process, the client generates the private key, while the CA generates the corresponding public key.

Managing certificate templates

Each issued certificate from the CA must use a certificate template. Certificate templates define how certificates can be requested and used, and what the purpose of the certificate will be. In Enterprise CA, all certificate templates that are configured are stored in the AD DS configuration partition. There are several versions of certificate templates that are related to the different versions of Windows Server operating systems. In Windows Server 2016, certificate templates version 4 and older are fully supported. Certificate templates are separated into two categories: for computers and for users. You can update certificate templates, copy templates, and supersede existing certificate templates.

Certificate templates allow administrators to customize certificate purposes, distribution methods, and other settings. The **Discretionary Access Control List (DACL)**, which is associated with each certificate template, defines the security permissions, or which security principals have permissions to read, enroll, or configure certificate templates. In Enterprise CA, certificate template permissions, as well as certificate templates, are stored in AD DS. If you have more than one CA in a AD DS forest, changes to permissions will be applied to all CAs.

A certification authority in Windows Server 2016 supports four versions of certificate templates. Version 4 is the default for Windows Server 2016, but this depends on the version of the Window Server operating system. Different versions of certificate templates have different functionalities:

- **Version 1**: This version is the default version for certificate templates when you install a CA. Changing permissions is only allowed on this version of certificate templates.
- **Version 2**: Some preconfigured certificate templates in a CA are version 2. If you want to support auto-enrollment, you need to create a version 2 certificate template.
- **Version 3**: This version supports **Cryptography Next Generation (CNG)**. CNG provides support for elliptic curve cryptography. If you use a version 3 certificate template, you can use CNG for certificates.
- **Version 4**: This is available only to Windows Server 2012 or Windows 8 operating systems and later. Version 4 certificate templates support both **cryptographic service providers (CSPs)** and key storage providers. You can also configure them to require renewal with the same key.

One of the first tasks in configuring certificate templates is defining permissions using the **Security** tab for each certificate template that you want to configure:

1. Open the **Certification Authority** console.
2. Expand **RootCA**, right-click on **Certificate Templates**, and click **Manage**:

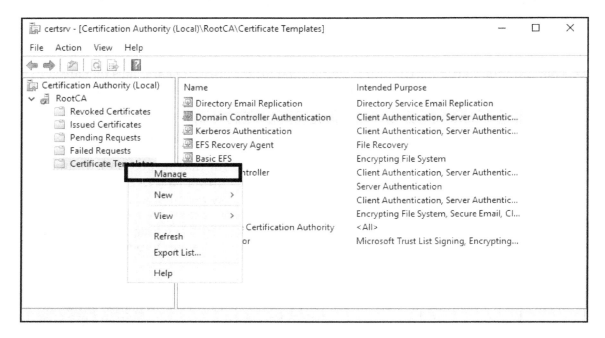

3. Once the **Certificate Templates** console is opened, select the desired certificate template, right-click, and select **Properties**.
4. Select the **Security** tab, and configure permissions according to your requirements:

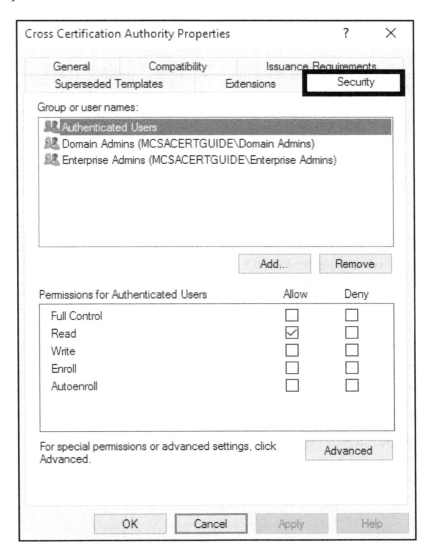

You can define the following permissions for certificate templates:

- **Full Control**: Allows a security principal to modify all attributes of a certificate template.
- **Read**: Allows a user or computer to view the certificate template when enrolling for certificates.
- **Write**: Allows a user or computer to modify the attributes of a certificate template.
- **Enroll**: Allows a user or computer to enroll for a certificate based on the certificate template.
- **Autoenroll**: Allows a user or computer to receive a certificate through the auto-enrollment process.

 Assigning permissions to groups is always a better approach than configuring permissions for individuals.

In some scenarios, you might need to reconfigure existing certificate templates or create new ones to meet the needs of an organization. For example, if you want to implement auto-enrollment of certificates, you need to have certificate template version 2 at least. To configure a certificate template, you need to define the following:

- The format and content of a certificate
- The process for creating and submitting a valid certificate request
- Which CSP is supported
- The key length and validity period
- The enrollment process and enrollment requirements

Based on the certificate's purpose, certificate templates are separated into two groups:

- **Single purpose**: Serves one purpose, such as allowing users to sign in with a smart card.
- **Multipurpose**: Serves more than one purpose at the same time, for example, a user certificate template serves multiple purposes by default.

Implementing and managing certificate deployment, validation, and revocation

One step in the process of implementing CAs is certificate distribution. It is also important to think about the revocation process, because in some scenarios you might need to revoke a certificate.

Windows Server 2016 supports several methods for user or computer certificate enrollment. Depending on scenario and certificate template version, you need to choose one of these enrollment methods:

- **Auto-enrollment**: This method requires certificate template version 2 or higher. Auto-enrollment permissions needs to be configured in the certificate template DACL. Using this method, the complete process will be done without user interaction and will need to be configured using the GPO.
- **Manual enrollment**: In this method, the user needs to request certificates using **Certificate Snap-in** or the `certreq` command-line tool. The private key and certificate request will be generated on a computer and transferred to a CA to generate a certificate, which will be transferred back and installed on the computer.
- **Web enrollment**: By using this method, the certificate needs to be requested by the website. The CA needs to have installed the CA Web Enrollment role service.
- **Enrollment on behalf**: In the first place, you must first create an Enrollment Agent, which is a user account used to request certificates on behalf of another user account.

The most efficient enrollment method is auto-enrollment. As mentioned, this method provides an automated method of certificate deployment to users and computers in an organization that has an AD DS forest infrastructure. The majority of certificate templates are, by default, version 1, which don't support auto-enrollment. Because of this, you need to duplicate the certificate template and configure permissions to support auto-enrollment. Then, you need to enable and activate auto-enrollment using Group Policy by configuring user or computer settings.

To configure certificate templates that support auto-enrollment, you need to follow these steps:

1. Open the **Certification Authority** console.
2. Expand the root CA, right-click on **Certificate Templates**, and click **Manage**.
3. Once the **Certificate Templates** console is opened, select the desired certificate template, right-click, and select **Duplicate Template**.

4. Define the certificate template properties based on your requirements.
5. Go to the **Security** tab, select the security principal, and check the **Autoenroll** checkbox:

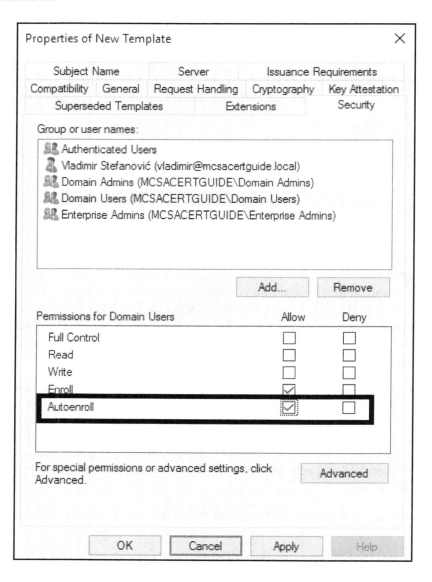

In GPO, you need to configure the **Certificate Services Client – Certificate Enrollment Policy** and **Certificate Services Client – Auto-Enrollment** settings under **Computer Configuration** | **Policies** | **Windows Settings** | **Security Settings** | **Public Key Policies** for computers and the same settings under **User Configuration** | **Policies** | **Windows Settings** | **Security Settings** | **Public Key Policies** for users:

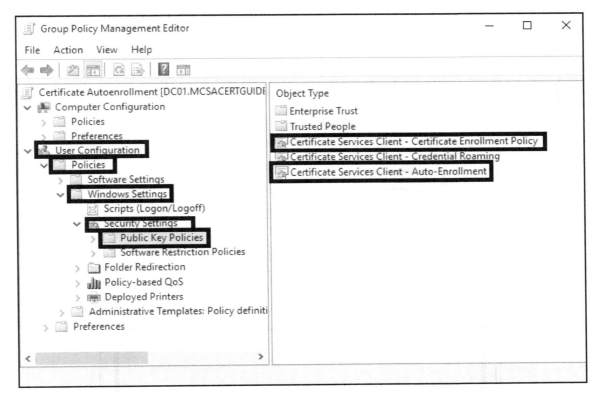

 Eight hours after enabling and configuring auto-enrollment for certificates, the auto-enrollment process will be triggered. If the user or computer has already got certificates issued using auto-enrollment, the certificate will not be issued again.

In some scenarios, you might need to revoke certificates. During the revocation process, the CA will disable the validity of the certificate. By initiating this process, the certificate's thumbprint will be published to the CRL, which will announce that the certificate is no longer valid. Publishing to a CRL is most important step in this process, because using the CRL is part of a certificate's validity.

Whenever a certificate needs to be used for any reason, the CRL needs to be contacted to check the certificate's validity. If the certificate is not on the CRL, the certificate consumer assumes that the certificate is not compromised and that it can be used without any consequences. If the certificate is on the CRL list, the certificate consumer will be warned that the certificate is not valid.

Earlier in this chapter, we described the importance of CRL and AIA access.

Once you open CRL, in the **Revocation List** tab, you can see the certificates that are revoked:

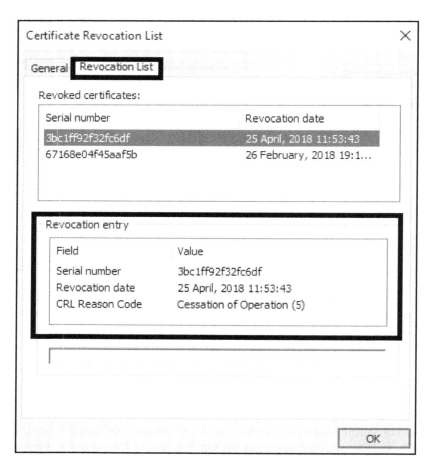

Managing certificate renewal

One of the management tasks in the PKI environment is certificate renewal. Like users and computers, the CA server has certificates that also need to be renewed. During the configuration of the CA server, you need to define the validity period and the key length. Although it is not recommended to use a long period of time for the validity period for CA servers, for root CA servers, you can define a longer period than the default (five years) and create a longer key length for better security. This is only acceptable if you have implemented a two-tier PKI infrastructure, because your root CA server will be offline most of the time. For a subordinate CA or a single CA, it is highly recommended to renew the certificate with a new key six to 12 months before the end of the CA's validity period. When a key is renewed, the CA will begin to publish a separate CRL for the revoked certificates. It will also continue to publish the CRL for certificates signed with the old key, as long as the validity period of these certificates is valid. For user and computer certificates, this process, along with the enrollment process, can be automated. If you have a certificate that is issued based on a version 4 certificate template, you can also configure it to require renewal with the same key.

Managing AD CS

In some scenarios, such as if we were to reinstall an operating system, the certificate and the pair of keys might lost. In this case, users can experience problems, because encrypted data or emails will not be readable any longer. In this section, you will learn how to implement, configure, and manage key recovery.

Configuring and managing key archival and recovery

The process of archiving and recovering keys and certificates is very important in the PKI life cycle. There are various reasons why this information might get lost and your users might have issues with recovering encrypted data or emails. Basically, you can export a certificate with a private key and store it in a secure location, such as in removable media or on the cloud, but this action requires manual interaction and can take a lot of time.

There are a few reasons why a pair of keys might get lost:

- The user profile is corrupted or deleted.
- The operating system is reinstalled.
- The hard drive is corrupted.
- The computer is stolen.

To prevent potential issues caused by these scenarios, in Windows Server 2016, you can enable and configure the key archival process. To enable this functionality in CA, you need to enable it at the CA level, as well as on the desired certificate template. This functionality is not enabled by default and will be fully functional once you configure it. In other words, certificates that are issued before configuring this functionality will not be able to be recovered if they are lost. To enable key archiving, you need to define the **Key Recovery Agent (KRA)**. The KRA is a user that has issued a KRA certificate and can decrypt private keys. When you configure key archival, private keys will be encrypted in the AD CS database with the KRA's public key and only the KRA's private key is able to decrypt the data. To enable this functionality, you need to enroll a certificate based on the KRA template for one user, and once the certificate is issued, key archival will be enabled by importing the KRA's public key to CA. From that moment, each certificate that is issued based on a certificate template in which key archival is enabled will have stored a private key in the AD CS database and will be encrypted with the KRA's public key.

To enable this functionality using the CA console, you need to perform the following steps:

1. Open the **Certificate Authority** console.
2. Expand CA, right-click on **Certificate Templates**, select **Manage**, and the **Certification Template** console will be opened.
3. Right-click on the **Key Recovery Agent** certificate template and select **Properties**.
4. In the **Issuance Requirements** tab, uncheck the **CA Certificate Manager Approval** box:

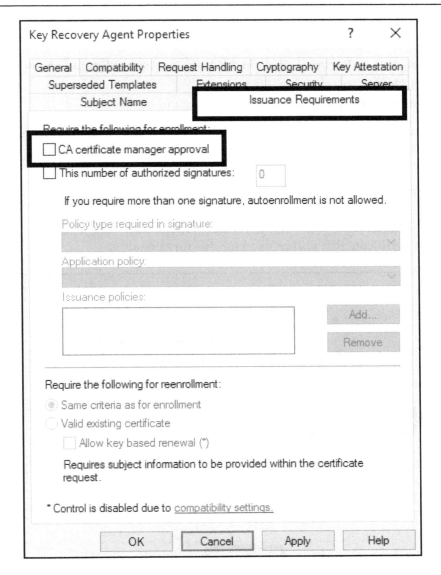

5. Close the **Certification Template** console.
6. Right-click on **Certificate Templates**, click on **New**, and select **Certification Template to Issue**.
7. Select **Key Recovery Agent** and click on **OK**.
8. Close the **Certificate Authority** console.
9. Open **MMC** by running mmc.exe in the Command Prompt or PowerShell.

10. Click *Ctrl + M* to add **Snap-in Certificates** for **My user account** and click **OK**.
11. Expand **Certificates – Current User**.
12. Right-click on **Personal**, click on **All tasks**, and select **Request New Certificate**.
13. Click **Next** twice.
14. Check the **Key Recovery Agent** checkbox and click **Enroll**.

After 20 to 30 seconds, the KRA certificate will be enrolled for the user. Then, you need to configure the properties of the CA and define which KRA certificate will be used in the key archival process:

1. Open the **Certificate Authority** console.
2. Right-click on the CA and select **Properties**.
3. In the **Recovery Agents** tab, select **Archive the key**, click **Add**, and select the KRA certificate that will be used for this functionality:

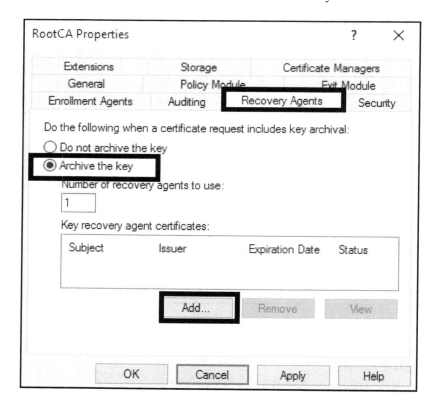

AD CS need to be rebooted to fully enable key archival.

After enabling and configuring KRA and key archival, all certificates that are issued based on a certificate template that supports key archival will be stored in the AD CS database and encrypted by the KRA's public key. By default, certificate templates don't support key archival, and you need to create a new certificate template to enable this functionality on the certificate template level:

1. Open the **Certificate Authority** console.
2. Expand CA, right-click on **Certificate Templates**, select **Manage**, and the **Certification Template** console will be opened.
3. Right-click on the desired certificate template and select **Duplicate Template**.
4. In the **Request Handling** tab, check **Archive subject's encryption private key**, and click **OK**:

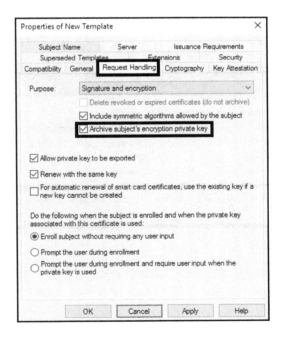

After these steps, your CA infrastructure will be fully configured for the key archival process. Private keys from issued certificates that are based on the configured certificate template will be stored in the AD CS database.

The key recovery process has two phases. In the first phase, a CA administrator needs to retrieve the encrypted file with the private key and certificate from the AD CS database. In the second phase, the KRA will decrypt the file and prepare the certificate and the private key for installation on the user or computer account. Before you start with the key recovery process, you need to obtain the serial key of the certificate:

1. Open the **Certificate Authority** console.
2. Select **Issued Certificates**, double-click on the desired certificate, and record the serial number from the **Details** tab:

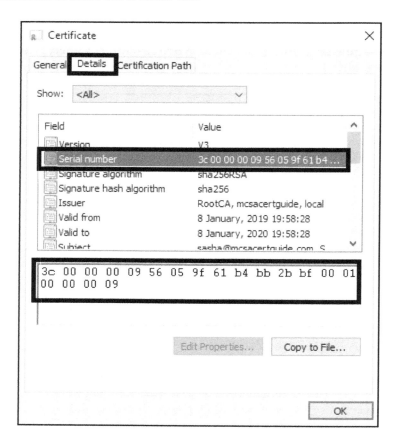

Once you have the serial number of the certificate that needs to be recovered, you need to run the following command in the Command Prompt or PowerShell:

```
Certutil –getkey <serial number> <OutputFileName>
```

Once you have the output file, you need to run the following command with the user that has the KRA certificate:

```
Certutil –recoverkey <OutputFileName> <CertificateName.pfx>
```

You need to enter a new certificate password twice. You will then have exported a certificate with a private key that is ready to import to the user or computer account.

Summary

Due to the importance of security, this chapter is also very important. In this chapter, you have learned about the concept of Public Key Infrastructure and how to install and configure a CA in Windows Server 2016. We have also described the difference between certificates and certificate templates, so you now know how to configure and manage both of these. Finally, you learned how to enable and configure the key archival process, and how to recover lost certificates and private keys.

Questions

1. What is the default certificate template version in Windows Server 2016?
    1. Version 2
    2. Version 1
    3. Version 4
    4. Version 3

2. What command needs to be used in the key recovery process?
    1. Ntdsutil
    2. Certutil
    3. Get-Certificate
    4. Recover-PrivateKey

3. Is RBAC supported for CA permissions?
    1. Yes
    2. No

4. Where is information about revoked certificates stored?
    1. AIA
    2. CRL
    3. CDP
    4. FTP

5. Which role service need to be used to check certificate validity using HTTP?
    1. Certificate Web Enrollment
    2. Online Responder
    3. AD CS
    4. Network Device Enrollment Service

6. Can a root CA server be offline?
    1. Yes
    2. No

7. Is auto-enrollment supported by default?
    1. Yes
    2. No

8. Which version of a certificate template is needed to support auto-enrollment?
    1. Version 2
    2. Version 1
    3. Version 4
    4. Version 3

Further reading

For further reading, please go to the following links:

- https://docs.microsoft.com/en-us/windows/desktop/seccertenroll/about-certification-authorities
- https://en.wikipedia.org/wiki/Public_key_infrastructure
- https://blogs.technet.microsoft.com/pki/2011/10/28/key-recovery-vs-data-recovery-differences/
- https://docs.microsoft.com/en-us/windows/desktop/seccertenroll/about-certificate-hierarchy

5
Understanding and Implementing Federation and Rights Management

Active Directory Federation Services (AD FS), a role in Windows Server 2016, gives you the ability to provide your users with authentication to external applications or services using their own local identities, managed by your AD DS. Another role that will be covered in this chapter is **Active Directory Rights Management Services (AD RMS)**, which helps you to protect your data in a different way to using BitLocker or an **Encrypting File System (EFS)**, or by configuring NTFS permissions of files and folders.

This chapter will show you how to implement, configure, and manage AD FS in different scenarios. We will also look at how to implement, configure, and manage the security of your data using AD RMS.

We will cover the following topics in this chapter:

- Installing and configuring **Active Directory Federation Services (AD FS)**
- Installing and configuring **Web Application Proxy (WAP)**
- Installing and configuring **Active Directory Rights Management Services (AD RMS)**

Installing and configuring Active Directory Federation Services (AD FS)

Due to the importance of federated identity in the modern world, it is vital to know how to implement, configure, and manage AD FS in Windows Server 2016. This section will cover some important aspects of AD FS management.

AD FS overview

AD FS is the default identity framework in Windows Server 2016. It allows you to establish trusts and share resources beyond AD DS boundaries. AD FS is compatible with common web service standards and can be used in various different scenarios. The identity federation service allows you to provide complete authentication mechanisms (identification, authentication, and authorization) beyond organizational boundaries. If you want to implement identity federation, both federation partners need to have created federation trusts. In the federated trust, each partner needs to define which resources will be made accessible to other organizations. You can also implement identity federation in a single organization, which comes in handy, for example, if you have implemented a web application that requires authentication. AD FS gives you the ability to implement authentication solutions for applications and makes it easy for users to authenticate with their AD DS credentials.

As mentioned, AD FS is the Microsoft implementation of an identity federation solution that uses claims-based authentication. The key features in Windows Server 2016 AD FS include the following:

- **Web Single Sign-On (SSO)**: Extends the ability to support authentication based on AD DS tokens to web applications.
- **Passive and smart client support**: Provides communication between passive clients, such as servers or browsers, as well as smart clients, such as mobile devices or applications.
- **Extensible architecture**: Supports various security token types, including **Security Assertion Markup Language (SAML)** tokens and Kerberos authentication. AD FS also supports the ability to convert one type of token to another.

Upgrading and migrating AD FS workloads to Windows Server 2016

Before you start installing and configuring AD FS, you need to understand the following AD FS components:

- **Federation server**: Issues, manages, and validates requests involving identity claims. AD FS implementation requires at least one federation service.
- **Federation service proxy**: An optional component that is deployed in the perimeter network. In Windows Server 2016, the federation server proxy functionality is part of the WAP.

- **Claims**: A statement that is made and claimed by a trusted entity that can include different types of attributes, based on scenarios wherever they are used.
- **Claims rules**: Determine how federation servers process claims.
- **Attribute store**: AD FS needs to check claim values in an attribute store. The most common attribute store is AD DS, because AD FS needs to be installed on a domain-joined server.
- **Claims provider**: A server that issues claims and authenticates users.
- **Relying parties**: A web service that consumes claims that are issued from the claims provider.
- **Claims provider trust**: Defines rules under which the client can request claims and submit them to the relying party.
- **Relying party trust**: Contains AD FS configuration that is used to provide claims about a client to the relying party.
- **Certificates**: AD FS communicates over the **Secure Sockets Layer** (**SSL**) and certificates are mandatory.

AD FS also has the following prerequisites for installation:

- All federation servers must be on domain-joined servers.
- The client computer must be able to communicate with the AD FS of the Web Proxy server using HTTPS.
- The Web Proxy server must be able to communicate with AD FS using HTTPS. The Web Proxy server doesn't need to be a domain-joined server.
- Federation servers and internal clients must be able to communicate with AD DS.

More information about AD FS prerequisites can be found at the following link: https://docs.microsoft.com/en-us/windows-server/identity/ad-fs/overview/ad-fs-requirements.

Installing AD FS

Once you meet all the prerequisites, you can start installing and configuring the AD FS server. You can do this using the Server Manager console, just like when adding other roles or features, or by using the PowerShell command. The PowerShell command that needs to be used for AD FS installation is as follows:

```
Install-WindowsFeature ADFS-Federation -IncludeManagementTools -
IncludeAllSubFeature
```

Once installed, the AD FS role needs to be configured before you start to use it. The configuration can be performed using the Server Manager console by starting post-deployment configuration:

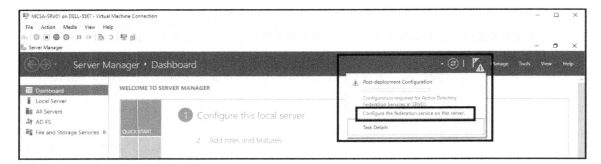

The following steps need to be performed if you want to create a new federation server farm:

1. On the welcome page, select **Create the first federation server in a federation server farm**.
2. On the **Connect to AD DS** page, define the administrator account.
3. On the **Specify Server Properties** page, select the appropriate **SSL Certificate** and **Federation Service Display Name**.

 You need to have a valid trusted SSL certificate for production in AD FS. In this example, I have used a self-signed certificate created by the following PowerShell command: `New-SelfSignedCertificate -DnsName adfs.mcsacertguide.local -CertStoreLocation Cert:\LocalMachine\My`. To avoid SSL warnings, you need to export the SSL certificate and then import it to the client machines and servers.

4. On the **Specify Service Account** page, define the service account or MSA that will be used for the AD FS service.
5. On the **Specify Database** page, define the parameters for the database connection.

If you want to perform AD FS configuration using PowerShell, you need to run the following command:

```
Install-AdfsFarm-CertificateThumbprint <ThumbPrintOfAdfsCertificate>-
FederationServiceDisplayName <ADFSServiceDisplayName>-FederationServiceName
<ServiceName>
```

The Federation Service Name must match the certificate name. Also, after running this command, you will be asked to add the service account credentials. Credentials need to be added in the following format: `DomainName\AccountName`.

Upgrading AD FS

If you have AD FS on Windows Server 2012 R2 and want to enable new functionalities in AD FS in Windows Server 2016, you need to perform a migration of AD FS. Although in many cases this is called upgrading, the complete process needs to be managed as migration. The following steps need to be performed:

1. Install a new Windows Server 2016 and install the AD FS role on that server.
2. During configuration, you need to add a new AD FS server to the existing federation server farm.
3. Move all AD FS roles to the new server using the following PowerShell command:

   ```
   Set-AdfsSyncProperties -Role PrimaryComputer
   ```

4. On the old AD FS server, run the following PowerShell command to set that server as a secondary AD FS server in the farm:

   ```
   Set-AdfsSyncProperties -PrimaryComputerName
   <NewPrimaryADFSServerName> -Role SecondaryComputer
   ```

5. Finally, upgrade the AD FS farm to the latest version, which is called the **Behavior Level**, by running the following PowerShell command:

   ```
   Invoke-AdfsFarmBehaviorLevelRaise
   ```

   For more information regarding upgrading AD FS versions, please use the following links:

   - https://docs.microsoft.com/en-us/windows-server/identity/ad-fs/deployment/upgrading-to-ad-fs-in-windows-server
   - https://docs.microsoft.com/en-us/windows-server/identity/ad-fs/deployment/upgrading-to-ad-fs-in-windows-server-sql

Implementing claim-based authentication and relying party trust

As mentioned earlier, an AD FS claim is a statement that a claims provider makes about an object, such as a user. The claims provider creates the claims and the relying party consumes the claims. The claim information provides the details that applications require to enable access to claims-aware applications. The email address, the UPN, or the last name are types that can be used for claims. AD FS provides a lot of built-in claim types, and you can create new ones based on your organization's needs. As the first step in AD FS planning, you need to define which types of claims and information your application needs to have to provide user access to the application. As mentioned, AD FS can obtain the necessary information to populate claims in a few different ways:

- Retrieve the claim from an attribute store
- Calculate the claim based on the information collected
- Transform the claim from one value to another
- Transform a Dynamic Access Control device claim into an AD FS claim

Another important thing to consider is claim rules. Claim rules define how claims are sent to and consumed by AD FS servers. You can use claim rules to define which incoming claims will be accepted from claims providers and which outbound claims will be provided to relying parties. Claim rules define how to apply authorization rules in order to enable access to the relying party for users or groups. In general, there are two different types of claim rules:

- **Claim rules for a claims provider trust**: Defines how the claims provider processes and issues claims
- **Claim rules for a relying party trust**: Defines how the relying party accepts claims from the claims provider

AD FS servers are preconfigured with a set of default rules and several default templates that you can use to create common claim rules.

Claims provider trust identifies the claims provider and describes how the relying party consumes the claims issued. Claims provider trust needs to be configured on each claim provider, and trust for local AD DS is configured by default. You need to create additional claims provider trusts when you configure AD FS to include other organizations.

There are three ways in which you can configure claims provider trust:

- Import data about the claims provider through the federation metadata
- Import data about the claims provider from a file
- Configure the claims provider trust manually

The relying party trust identifies the relying party and defines the claim rules that define how the relying party accepts and processes claims from the claims provider. In a single organization, the relying party trust will define how AD FS interacts with applications, and in the configuration process you just need to provide the URL of an application. If you want to include other organizations in AD FS, you need to create additional relying party trusts for each organization. Like claim provider trust, there are three different options:

- Import data about the relying party through the federation metadata
- Import data about the relying party from a file
- Configure the relying party trust manually

 In the following example, the internal application will be configured for AD FS. The server that hosts the application must have installed **Web Server (IIS)** and Windows Identity Foundation 3.5. Windows Identity Foundation SDK, which can be downloaded from https://www. microsoft.com/download/details.aspx?id=4451, also needs to be installed. A simple application can be downloaded from https://1drv. ms/u/s!AvyV-qb5pRmgi6gyWYThw-Grj9XoKQ and needs to be added to IIS.

To configure the Active Directory claims provider trust, you need to perform the following steps. All tasks need to be performed on the AD FS server:

1. Open the **AD FS Management** console.
2. Expand **Claims Provider Trusts**, right-click on **Active Directory**, and then click **Edit Claim Rules**.
3. On the **Acceptance Transform Rules** tab, click **Add Rule**.
4. On the **Choose Rule Type** step, select **Send LDAP Attributes as Claims** and then click **Next**.
5. In the **Configure Claim Rule** step, define the rule name and select **Active Directory** as the **Attribute store**.

6. In the same step, define the mappings shown in the screenshot and click **Finish**:

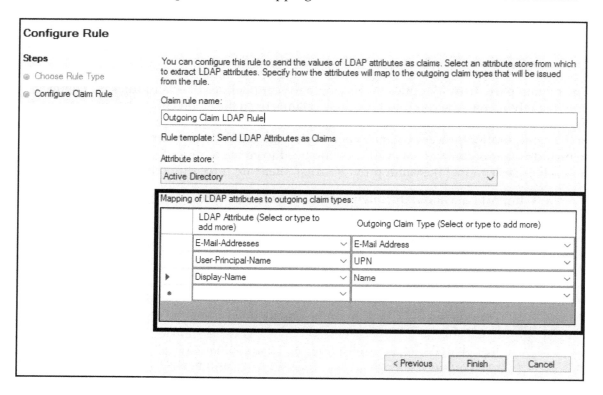

 In this example, the application is stored at the location `C:\inetpub\wwwroot\TestApp`. Application binding is configured as `TestApp.mcsacertguide.local`.

On the server where the application is installed, you need to configure the application to trust incoming claims, as follows:

1. Open the **Windows Identity Foundation Federation Utility** console.
2. On the **Welcome to the Federation Utility Wizard** page, in the **Application configuration location** box, type
   `C:\inetpub\wwwroot\TestApp\web.config` and `https://testapp.mcsace rtguide.local/`.
3. On the **Security Token Service** page, click **Use an existing STS**, and in the STS WS-Federation metadata document location box, type
   `https://adfs.mcsacertguide.local/federationmetadata/2007-06/fed erationmetadata.xml`.
4. On the **STS signing certificate chain validation error** page, click **Disable certificate chain validation**.
5. On the **Security token encryption** page, click **No encryption**.
6. On the **Offered claims** page, click **Next**.
7. On the **Summary** page, click **Finish**.

To configure a relying party trust for the claims-aware application, we need to perform the following steps. All tasks need to be performed on the AD FS server:

1. Open the **AD FS Management** console.
2. Right-click on **Relying Party Trusts**, and select **Add Relying Party Trust**.
3. On the **Welcome** page, select **Claims aware**.
4. On the **Selected Data Source** page, select **Import data about the relying party published online or on a local network** and type
   `https://testapp.mcsacertguide.local/federationmetadata/2007-06/ federationmetadata.xml` in the **Federated metadata address** box.
5. On the **Specify Display Name** page, define the name of the relying party.
6. On the **Choose Access Control Policy** page, click **Next**.
7. On the **Ready to Add Trust** page, click **Next**.
8. On the **Finish** page, ensure that **Configure claims issuance policy for this application** is checked and click **Close**.

To configure the claim rules for the relying party trust, perform the following steps on the AD FS server:

1. Open the **AD FS Management** console.
2. Expand **Relying Party Trusts**, right-click on the previously created relying party trust, and select **Edit Claim Issuance policy**.
3. On the **Issuance Transform Rules** tab, click **Add Rule**.

4. On the **Choose Rule Type** page, select **Pass Through or Filter an Incoming Claim**.

5. On the **Configure Claim Rule** page, type **Pass through Windows account name** in the **Claim rule name** box and select **Windows account name** in the **Incoming claim type** list.

6. On the **Choose Rule Type** page, select **Pass Through or Filter an Incoming Claim**.

7. On the **Configure Claim Rule** page, type **Pass through E-Mail Address** in the **Claim rule name** box and select **E-Mail Address** in the **Incoming claim type** list.

8. On the **Choose Rule Type** page, select **Pass Through or Filter an Incoming Claim**.

9. On the **Configure Claim Rule** page, type **Pass through UPN** in the **Claim rule name** box and select **UPN** in the **Incoming claim type** list.

10. On the **Choose Rule Type** page, select **Pass Through or Filter an Incoming Claim**.

11. On the **Configure Claim Rule** page, type **Pass through Name** in the **Claim rule name** box and select **Name** in the **Incoming claim type** list.

In the end, you need to validate your work. Open the client machine and type in the browser application URL in the format `https://testapp.mcsacertguide.local/`. If everything is configured properly and you provide credentials in the format `DomainName\AccountName`, you will see the claim information, as shown in the following screenshot:

If you receive the error message **The data protection operation was unsuccessful. This may have been caused by not having the user profile loaded for the current thread's user context, which may be the case when the thread is impersonating** during the validation process, you need to reconfigure the application pool that is used for your claims-aware application. You need to do the following:

1. Open **IIS Manager**.
2. Expand **Application Pools**, right-click on the application pool that is used for the application, and select **Advanced Settings**.
3. Find the **Process Model** section in options and change the parameter for **Load User Profile** to **True**:

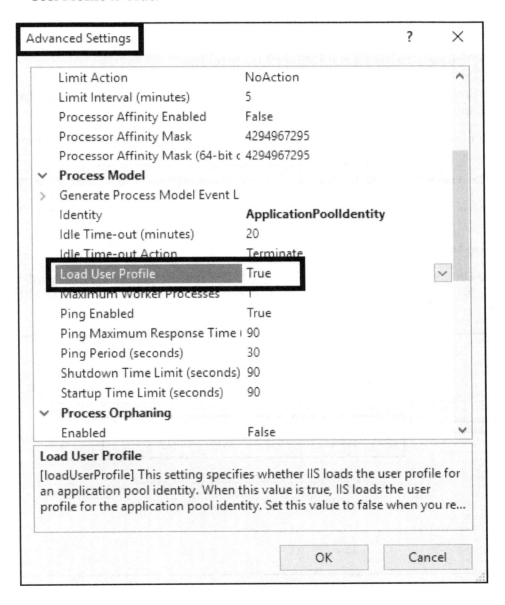

Implementing and configuring device registration

From Windows Server 2012 R2, in the AD FS server, we implement the **Device Registration Service (DRS)**. The DRS is included in the AD FS role, but must be installed and configured on all AD FS servers in your farm before you use it. This feature gives you the ability to authenticate devices via the Workplace Join process.

There are two prerequisites for a successful implementation of DRS:

- You need to have a valid SSL certificate for the `enterpriseregistration.domain.com`
- You need to have a DNS record for enterprise registration that needs to point to the IP address of the name of the AD FS server

Once you meet these prerequisites, you need to run the following PowerShell command on the AD FS server that will initialize the DRS feature:

```
Initialize-ADDeviceRegistration -ServiceAccountName <ServiceAccountName>
```

When DRS is initialized, you need to run the following PowerShell command to enable the feature:

```
Enable-AdfsDeviceRegistration
```

When the DRS is enabled, a new container in AD DS, called registered devices, will be created. Also, in the AD FS Management console, you will be able to see that the DRS is enabled:

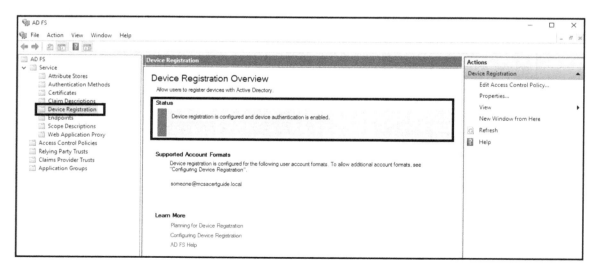

Once the DRS is enabled, it gives you the ability to perform Workplace Join on the client machines that run Windows 8.1 or later. When a machine is successfully registered to DRS, you will be able to see the new object in AD DS, under the **RegisteredDevices** container:

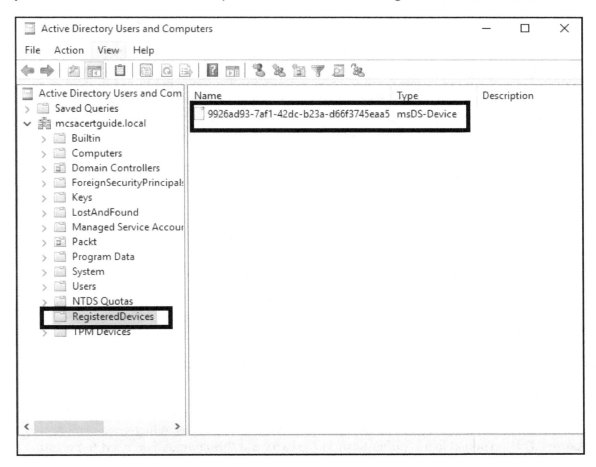

 Ensure that you have checked the **Device Authentication** checkbox in **Primary Authentication Methods**. To configure this option, you need to open the **AD FS Management** console, expand **Authentication Methods** under **Service**, and select **Edit Primary Authentication Methods** in the **Action** pane.

Configuring AD FS for use with Microsoft Azure and Office 365

In the cloud era, many organizations use some cloud services in a hybrid environment. The most common scenario is to use Office 365 as a mail solution, as well as all other cloud applications that use Azure AD for authentication, with implemented directory synchronization and local AD DS.

In this scenario, anytime users want to open a cloud application using their browser, such as Outlook or OneDrive, they will be asked to enter their credentials, even though they use the same credentials for on-premises and cloud environments. AD FS can provide identity mechanisms for cloud-based applications and give you the ability to configure SSO experience.

Before you start this process, the following points are mandatory:

- The user's UPN needs to be the same in both environments, on-premises and in the cloud
- The AD FS server needs to be reachable from the internet on port 443

 To avoid potential security issues by making the AD FS server reachable from the internet, you can install and configure the WAP. This will be described in the following section of this chapter.

The first step in this process is to install and configure the AD FS server. Once you have configured the federation server farm, you need to enable PowerShell remoting on the AD FS server. This can be done using the PowerShell `Enable-PSRemoting` command. When you configure PowerShell remoting on the AD FS server, you need to configure your cloud side. Your Office 365/Azure domain needs to be configured as a Federated domain. By default, all domains configured in the cloud are Standard domains, which means that Azure AD is responsible for authentication. To carry out this change, you need to perform the following steps:

1. Log in to the Microsoft Online service using the PowerShell `Connect-MsolService` command with global admin credentials.

2. Run the `Set-MsolADFSContext -Computer <AD FS Server FQDN>` command to configure the AD FS context in the cloud.

3. Run the `Convert-MsolDomainToFederated -DomainName <DomainName>` command to convert your domain from Standard to Federated.

Don't connect to Office 365/Azure AD with an account that has a domain that needs to be federated. Use the global admin account configured with the default @domain.onmicrosoft.com domain or any other domain that will not be federated.

Depending on the number of users, this process might take up to 30 minutes.

Installing and configuring Web Application Proxy

If your organization has an application that uses AD FS for authentication and needs to be reachable from the internet, exposing AD FS to the internet is not the best idea. In this scenario, achieving security and authentication goals requires some type of reverse proxy. In Windows Server 2016, you can use the **Windows Application Proxy (WAP)** to make your internal application reachable from the internet in a secure manner. In this section, you will learn how to install and configure WAP for AD FS workloads.

Installing and configuring WAP

WAP is a role service in Windows Server 2016 that helps you to secure remote access to web-based applications in your organization. WAP can work as a reverse proxy, as well as an AD FS proxy. From a security perspective, WAP should be placed in the perimeter network and provide web access to external clients. WAP is responsible for establishing connections to web applications or AD FS on the internal network. Web clients don't need any specific configurations for using WAP.

WAP is a role service that is part of the Remote Access role and can be installed using the Server Manager console or PowerShell. The installation process is straightforward, but if you want to install it using the Server Manager console, you need to select **Remote Access** for installation and later in the wizard select **Web Application Proxy** on the page for selecting **Role Services** for installation, as shown in the following screenshot:

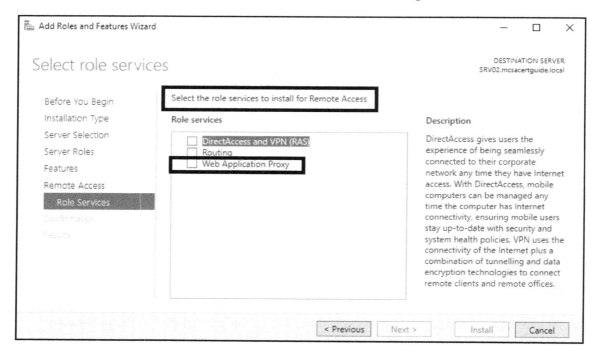

If you want to use PowerShell, you need to run the following command:

```
Install-WindowsFeature Web-Application-Proxy -IncludeAllSubFeature -
IncludeManagementTools
```

Before you start with the WAP configuration, you need to meet some prerequisites, especially if you want to implement WAP as an AD FS proxy:

- **Certificate**: The same certificate that is installed and used for AD FS needs to be installed to WAP because WAP is the connection point for external clients. This cannot be done during installation, so you need to export the certificate from the AD FS server, import it to the WAP server, and select the certificate during configuration.
- **Load Balancing**: Like web applications, you can implement Network Load Balancing for two or more WAP servers, if you need to have redundancy for WAP servers.
- **DNS**: Because WAP needs to be implemented in the perimeter network, you need to properly configure all the necessary DNS records, so that WAP can reach the servers in the internal network, such as AD FS or the web application server.

Once you have installed WAP on Windows Server 2016, you need to perform post-configuration:

1. On the **Federation Server** page, you need to define the federation service name and the account with local admin credentials on the AD FS server.

 If you are not sure about the federation service name, you can check in the AD FS Management console on AD FS server. When you open the **AD FS Management** console, right-click on **Service** and select **Edit Federation Service Properties**. On the **General** tab, you can find the **Federation Service name**.

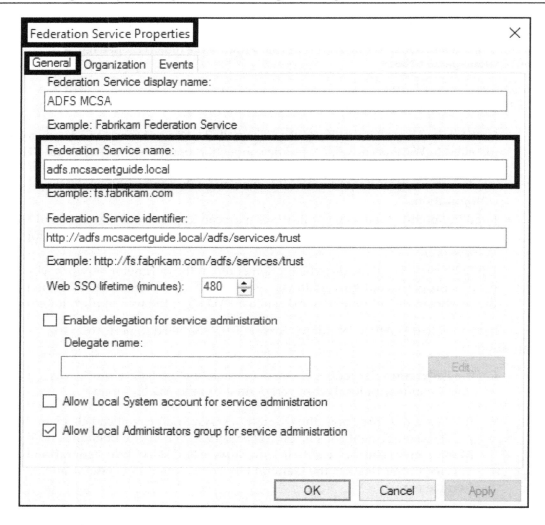

2. On the **AD FS Proxy Certificate** page, select the previously imported certificate from the AD FS server.

3. On the **Confirmation** page, click **Configure**.

If you want to use PowerShell to configure WAP, you need to run the following commands:

```
$Credentials = Get-Credential
Install-WebApplicationProxy -FederationServiceTrustCredential $Credentials
-CertificateThumbprint <ADFSCertificateThumbprint> -FederationServiceName
<FerderationServiceName>
```

When you configure WAP, you need to reboot the WAP server in order to have a functional WAP.

Implementing WAP in pass-through mode and as AD FS proxy

As mentioned, WAP needs to be used when you want to protect an AD FS web application that is accessible from the internet. Once configured, all the configuration information is stored in the AD FS database and it is a functional as AD FS proxy. In other words, all AD FS authentication requests that come to WAP will be forwarded to AD FS. However, if you want to configure WAP for web applications, you need to configure each application in WAP and select from two pre-authentication methods: pass-through and AD FS pre-authentication.

Pass-through pre-authentication

When you configure a web application to use pass-through pre-authentication, valid requests will be passed to web-based applications without performing user authentication. In other words, the application is responsible for user authentication. Pre-authentication can protect a web application from a DoS attack but cannot be protected from application-level threats. To configure pass-through pre-authentication, you need to follow the steps listed here:

1. Open the **Remote Access Management** console.
2. Under **Configuration**, select **Web Application Proxy** and select **Publish** under **Tasks**. A new wizard, **Publish New Application**, will be opened:

3. On the **Pre-authentication** page, select **Pass-through**.
4. On the **Publishing Settings** page, you need to define the name, the external and internal URLs, and the external certificate for the application.
5. On the **Confirmation** page, click **Publish**.

In the following screenshot, you can see the configuration parameters from my test application, where I have configured the same external and internal URL. I also wanted to force the clients to use HTTPS by enabling HTTP-to-HTTPS redirection:

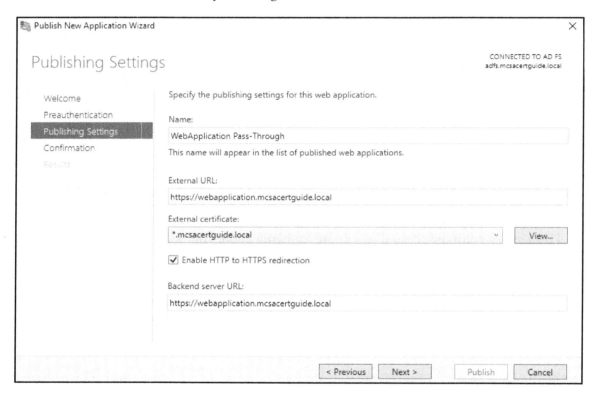

If you want to publish a web application with the same settings using PowerShell, you need to run the following command:

```
Add-WebApplicationProxyApplication -BackendServerUrl <BackendURL> -
ExternalCertificateThumbprint <CertificateThimbprint> -
EnableHTTPRedirect:$true -ExternalUrl <ExternalURL> -Name <PublishName> -
ExternalPreAuthentication PassThrough
```

AD FS pre-authentication

The other option to configure pre-authentication is AD FS pre-authentication. When you configure AD FS as the pre-authentication method, AD FS authenticates a user request before passing it to the web application. In this scenario, only the authorized users can send requests to the web application. AD FS pre-authentication provides a better level of web application security. The limitation of AD FS, however, is that only claims-aware applications that use AD FS for authentication can use AD FS pre-authentication.

 In this example, I have used a claims-aware application that was configured in the previous section.

To configure the AD FS pre-authentication method, you need to perform the following steps:

1. Open the **Remote Access Management** console.
2. Under **Configuration**, select **Web Application Proxy** and select **Publish** under **Tasks**. A new wizard, **Publish New Application**, will be opened.
3. On the **Pre-authentication** page, select **Active Directory Federation Services (AD FS)**.
4. On the **Supported Clients** page, select **Web and MSOFBA**.
5. On the **Relying Party** page, select an application that has been configured previously.
6. On the **Publishing Settings** page, you need to define the name, the external and internal URLs, and the external certificate for the application.
7. On the **Confirmation** page, click **Publish**.

If you want to publish web applications with the same settings using PowerShell, you need to run the following command:

```
Add-WebApplicationProxyApplication -BackendServerUrl <BackendURL> -
ExternalCertificateThumbprint <CertificateThumbprint> -
EnableHTTPRedirect:$true -ExternalUrl <ExternalURL> -Name <PublishingName>
-ExternalPreAuthentication ADFS -ADFSRelyingPartyName <RelyingPartyName>
```

Publishing Remote Desktop Gateway applications

In some scenarios, an organization might want to implement Remote Desktop services for publishing applications or desktops via web access. If some Remote Desktop scenarios include external access, configuring **Remote Desktop Gateway** (**RD Gateway**) role services is highly recommended. Implementing RD Gateway with WAP provides access restriction and adds pre-authentication for remote users. This can be accomplished by using either pre-authentication method. Here are the methods:

- **Publishing using pass-through authentication**: Provides a single point of entry into your Remote Desktop environment. The configuration might vary depending on your Remote Desktop infrastructure.
- **Publishing by using pre-authentication**: You need to add relying party trust to enforce clients to use pre-authentication. When a client wants to authenticate to the Remote Desktop Gateway, the application will respond with a message that pre-authentication is required.

Installing and configuring the Active Directory Rights Management Services (AD RMS)

Active Directory Rights Management Services (**AD RMS**), a protection technology that is part of Windows Server, allows you to protect your data in a different way to NTFS or EFS/Bitlocker. The main purpose of AD RMS is to prevent data leakage. It can be integrated with Microsoft services, such as Microsoft Exchange or Microsoft SharePoint, as well as Office 365 services. In this section, you will learn how to implement and configure AD RMS in your organization.

AD RMS overview

AD RMS can protect data in transit, as well as at rest. Unlike EFS, where your data is encrypted and protected by default, AD RMS gives you the ability to protect and share data with the possibility to provide additional options, such as automatically deleting messages or preventing users from saving or printing emails or documents.

The AD RMS infrastructure is a little bit confusing to understand and consists of a few different components. The most important component is the AD RMS root certification cluster, which is created by deploying the first AD RMS server in the environment. This component is responsible for managing all licensing and AD RMS certificates in the organization where it is installed. AD RMS stores all information in SQL or WID databases, and if you have a large environment, the SQL server that hosts databases for AD RMS should be deployed on a separate server. As a component, AD RMS also consists of the following:

- **AD RMS server**: This must be a domain member. As mentioned, the first deployed AD RMS server will create an AD RMS cluster and the cluster information will be published in AD DS as a **Service Connection Point (SCP)** that will be used by clients to locate the AD RMS cluster.
- **AD RMS client**: By default, this is built into Windows Vista and later operating systems.
- **AD RMS enabled applications**: These are applications that allow a user to create AD RMS-protected content. By default, Office applications are AD RMS-enabled, but you can create your own AD RMS-enabled application using the AD RMS SDK.

AD RMS certificates

Before you start installing and using AD RMS, you need to know how it works. AD RMS uses a few different certificates, but you don't need to have Certificate Authority installed and configured. Certificates are a very important part of the AD RMS infrastructure:

- **Server licensor certificate**: This will be generated when you create an AD RMS cluster, with a validity period of 250 years. This certificate allows the AD RMS cluster to issue other certificates and policy templates.
- **AD RMS machine certificate**: This certificate will identify the client computer. With the certificate's public key, the **Right Account Certificate (RAC)** key will be encrypted and decrypted with the private key.

- **Right Account Certificate**: This identifies a specific user. The default validity of the RAC is one year and can be issued only to AD DS users that have an email address associated with an AD DS account. If a RAC needs to be issued to a user that is not a domain member, a temporary RAC will be issued with a validity of 15 minutes.
- **Client licensor certificate**: This allows the user to publish AD RMS-protected content when a computer is not connected to the same network as the AD RMS cluster. The client licensor certificate is strictly tied to the user's RAC.
- **Publishing license (PL)**: This defines the right that you have to an AD RMS-protected document.
- **End user license**: This license is required to consume AD RMS protected documents.

How AD RMS works

As mentioned, AD RMS has a bit of a different process to other services that use certificates. We have learned that AD RMS has a lot of certificates. The following steps will explain how the AD RMS workflow works:

1. When a user creates an AD RMS-protected document, the client licensor certificate will be requested from the AD RMS server, which is located using the service connection point in AD DS.
2. The AD RMS cluster will issue the client licensor certificate to the user.
3. Once the user receives the client licensor certificate from the AD RMS cluster, the usage rights can be configured manually or according to preconfigured templates.
4. When the usage rights are configured, the protected file will be encrypted using a symmetric key that is generated on the user's device and the document will be in an encrypted state.
5. The symmetric key will be encrypted using the public key of an AD RMS server that the user is using. This will be stored in the AD RMS database.
6. When the recipient receives the AD RMS-protected file, if they don't have the account certificate on the device, the file cannot be opened. The recipient's application or browser will send a request to the AD RMS server.
7. If the user is authorized to open an AD RMS-protected document, AD RMS will issue a use license to the recipient.
8. AD RMS will decrypt the symmetric key that is used to encrypt the document.

9. At the end of the process, AD RMS will encrypt the symmetric key with the recipient's use license public key and the key to use the license certificate that will be distributed to the recipient. The recipient will use the private key from the use license certificate to decrypt the symmetric key that is used to decrypt the AD RMS-protected document:

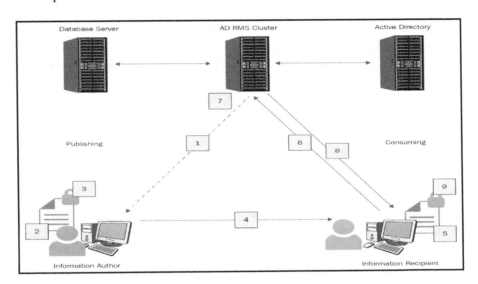

Deploying the AD RMS Cluster

As mentioned, by deploying the first AD RMS server in an infrastructure, you will create an AD RMS cluster. An AD RMS cluster is not a highly available cluster, like a failover cluster on Windows Server. In most cases, AD RMS is deployed on highly available virtual machines that are deployed on Hyper-V clusters. AD RMS can be deployed in a single forest, as well as in multiple forests. The single-forest implementation has a single AD RMS cluster. The multi-forest implementation needs to have an AD RMS cluster per forest, except in a scenario in which you have AD FS configured to use a single AD RMS cluster in multiple forests.

You can install AD RMS by using the Server Manager console or the following PowerShell command:

```
Install-WindowsFeature ADRMS-Server -IncludeAllSubFeature -
IncludeManagementTools
```

Once installed, the AD RMS server needs to be configured by post-deployment configuration before you start to use it:

1. On the **AD RMS Cluster** page, select **Create a new AD RMS root cluster**.
2. On the **Configuration Database** page, select **Use Windows Internal Database on this server**.
3. On the **Service Account** page, select a previously created service account.
4. On the **Cryptographic Mode** page, select **Cryptographic Mode 2**.
5. On the **Cluster Key Storage** page, select **Use AD RMS centrally managed key storage**.
6. On the **Cluster Key Password** page, define a strong password.
7. On the **Cluster Web Site** page, select the website at which you want to configure the cluster.
8. On the **Cluster Address** page, define the FQDN of the cluster website and protocol.

 HTTPS needs to be used if you plan to use Identity Federation Support. Also, once the FQDN and port are configured, they cannot be changed later. The DNS for FQDN needs to be configured, because it will not be added automatically.

9. On the **Licensor Certificate** page, define the name of the licensor certificate.
10. On the **SCP Registration** page, select **Register the SCP now**.
11. On the **Confirmation** page, click **Install**.

After installation, you need to log off and on again before you start to administer AD RMS.

Managing AD RMS Service Connection Point (SCP)

You have already learned that SCP allows AD RMS-enabled users to retrieve an AD RMS URL from AD DS. SCP can be registered during the configuration of the AD RMS cluster or later. Accounts that perform registration need to be members of Enterprise Admin groups. You can also modify the SCP properties after installation if the user account is a member of the AD RMS Enterprise Administrators group and the Enterprise Admins group:

1. Open the **Active Directory Right Management Services** console.
2. Right-click on the AD RMS server and select **Properties**..

3. On the **SCP** tab, check the **Change SCP** checkbox and you will be able to change the parameters:

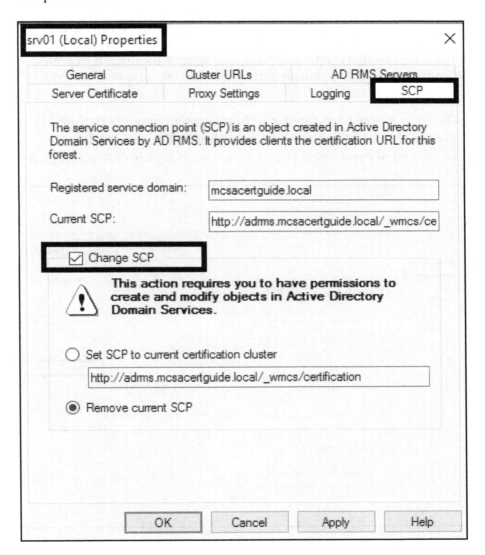

Managing AD RMS templates

Although AD RMS-enabled users can protect documents by manually configuring usage rights, templates allow you to configure standardized policies for organizations. For example, if you want to grant read-only permissions on a protected document, you can create a policy template that can be preconfigured when a user wants to protect a document. To create a new template or edit an existing one, you need to use the AD RMS console:

1. Open the **Active Directory Right Management Services** console.
2. Expand the AD RMS server and select **Rights Policy Template**.
3. In the **Action Pane**, select **Create Distributed Rights Policy Template**:

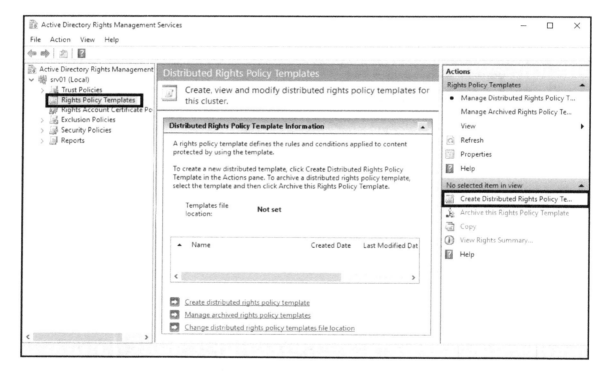

4. On the **Add Template Identification Information** page, click **Add** and define the language, name, and description of the policy template.

5. On the **Add User Right** page, define what permission users or groups will have when a document is protected with this template.

6. On the **Specify Expiration Policy** page, define when the content and license will expire.

7. On the **Specify Extended Policy** page, define the additional parameters of the policy, such as disabling client-side caching.

8. On the **Specify Revocation Policy** page, define whether documents protected with this template can be revoked and click **Finish**.

Once the policy template is configured, users will be able to use it when protecting documents.

Configuring Exclusion Policies

Exclusion Policies allow you to prevent specific users or apps from using AD RMS. Exclusions are disabled by default and need to be enabled before you configure them. User exclusion needs to be performed by excluding the RAC that is tied to the AD DS user account:

1. Open the **Active Directory Right Management Services** console.
2. Expand the AD RMS server and **Exclusion Policies** and select **Users**.

3. In the **Actions** pane, click on **Enable User Exclusion**:

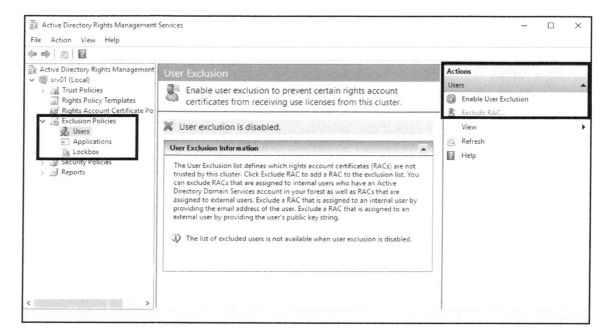

You will then be able to click on **Exclude RAC** and define the user accounts that will be excluded.

To perform application exclusion, you need to follow the steps given here:

1. Open the **Active Directory Right Management Services** console.
2. Expand the AD RMS server and the **Exclusion Policies** and select **Applications**.
3. In the **Actions** pane, click on **Enable Application Exclusion**.
4. In the **Actions** pane, click on **Exclude Application**.

In a new wizard, you need to enter information about the application that will be excluded from AD RMS:

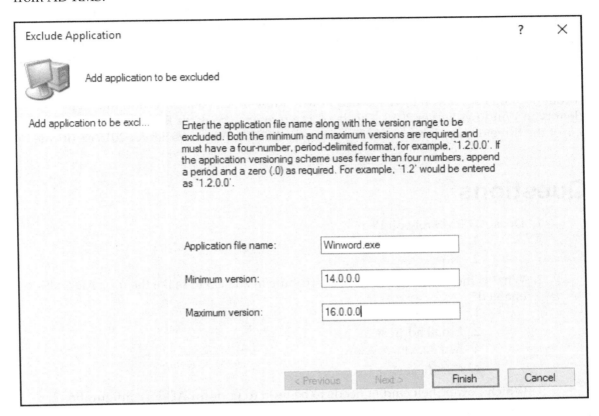

Backing up and restoring AD RMS

Like all other services in an organization, the AD RMS server needs to be backed up so you can restore it if it fails. Because it is recommended that you deploy AD RMS as a highly available virtual machine, the easiest and recommended way to back up the AD RMS server is by using some Enterprise software, such as System Center Data Protection Manager. You can also use Windows Server Backup to perform a full backup of the AD RMS server. Also, as a best practice, you should back up the AD RMS private key, all certificates that are used by AD RMS, the SQL database, and all AD RMS templates.

Summary

In the last chapter of this book, we have learned how to install and configure AD FS, how to configure claim-based applications to use AD FS authentication, and how to protect your web-based application. We have also learned that AD FS needs to be published on the internet using a WAP. Finally, we have looked at how to install and configure AD RMS and how to configure various policies to protect your information from data leakage.

Throughout this book, you have learned how to implement, configure, and maintain identity in Windows Server 2016. This book is a reference book for Exam 70-742, which is one of the three required exams for acquiring the MCSA: Windows Server 2016 certificate.

Questions

1. Does AD RMS rely on PKI?
   1. Yes
   2. No
2. What is the most important user attribute in AD DS to make the user AD RMS-enabled?
   1. Password
   2. Email address
   3. msDSRMS-Account
   4. Certificate
3. Which PowerShell cmdlet needs to be used to perform AD FS configuration?
   1. Set-Adfs
   2. Install-AdfsFarm
   3. Install-Adfs
   4. Set-AdfsFarm
4. Which two PowerShell cmdlets need to be performed to enable and configure Device Registration?
   1. Initialize-ADDeviceRegistration
   2. Enable-ADDeviceRegistration
   3. Set-AdfsDeviceRegistration
   4. Enable-AdfsDeviceRegistration

5. Which is a lower domain role that can register SCP for AD RMS?
    1. Server Operator
    2. Domain Administrator
    3. Enterprise Administrator
    4. AD RMS Administrator

6. What are the prerequisites to configure AD FS pre-authentication for web-based applications?
    1. Application must use only HTTPS
    2. Application need to be claims-aware
    3. Application must be on a server that is a domain member
    4. The Web Application Proxy needs to be in a perimeter network

7. Where will pass-through pre-authentication send the authentication?
    1. AD DS
    2. AD FS
    3. Application
    4. AD RMS

8. Which PowerShell cmdlets need to be used to configure AD FS for Office 365?
    1. `Convert-MsolDomainToFederated`
    2. `Configure-ADFSContext`
    3. `Set-MsolADFSContext`
    4. `Convert-MsolDomainToStandard`

Further reading

For further reading regarding the topics covered in this chapter, please use the following links:

- `https://blogs.technet.microsoft.com/rmilne/2017/04/28/how-to-install-ad-fs-2016-for-office-365/`
- `https://docs.microsoft.com/en-us/windows-server/remote/remote-access/web-application-proxy/web-application-proxy-windows-server`
- `https://docs.microsoft.com/en-us/azure/information-protection/develop/ad-rms-server`
- `https://docs.microsoft.com/en-us/windows-server/identity/ad-fs/overview/ad-fs-requirements`

Assessements

Chapter 1: Installing and Configuring Active Directory

1. Domain-naming master and Schema master
2. `Ntdsutil.exe`
3. Demote domain controller
4. Active Directory Users and Computers
5. No
6. Yes
7. Infrastructure master
8. No
9. Yes

Chapter 2: Managing and Maintaining Active Directory

1. No
2. 180 minutes
3. Create more than one password policy in the domain
4. The following statements to do with authoritative and non-authoritative restoration are correct:
     - Authoritative restoration can replicate recovered objects to other domain controllers
     - Non-authoritative restoration will be used in case one domain controller fails or gets corrupted

5. Yes
6. Stop the AD DS service and manage the AD DS database in offline mode
7. `Ntdsutil.exe`
8. Windows Server 2012 R2
9. Windows Server 2012 R2
10. No

Chapter 3: Creating and Managing Group Policy

1. Object nearest OU policy
2. Yes
3. Conditions that will be applied during the processing of GPOs
4. Merge and Replace
5. No
6. Yes
7. `Set-GPInherintace`
8. Filtering GPOs applying based on computer hardware or software

Chapter 4: Understanding and Implementing Active Directory Certificate Services

1. Version 1
2. Certutil
3. Yes
4. CRL
5. Online Responder
6. Yes
7. No
8. Version 2

Chapter 5: Understanding and Implementing Federation and Rights Management

1. Yes
2. Email address
3. `Install-AdfsFarm`
4. The two PowerShell cmdlets need to be performed to enable and configure Device Registration are as follows:
   - `Initialize-ADDeviceRegistration`
   - `Enable-ADDeviceRegistration`
5. Enterprise Administrator
6. Application need to be claims-aware
7. Application
8. PowerShell cmdlets need to be used to configure AD FS for Office 365 are as follows:
   - `Convert-MsolDomainToFederated`
   - `Set-MsolADFSContext`

Index

Made in the USA
Middletown, DE
15 July 2019